CW01022993

WALKING THE

PEAK WAY

KEN REECE

**Peak
Way**

© 2022 Peak Way Publishing
Published 2022
Text © Ken Reece

All photographs taken on the route by the author,
Ken Reece and Danny Reece

The moral right of Ken Reece to be identified as the author of
this work has been asserted by him in accordance with the
Copyright, Designs and Patents Act 1988.

All rights reserved. No part of this book may be reproduced or
utilised in any form or by any means, electronic or mechanical,
including photocopying, recording or by any information storage
and retrieval system, without permission in writing from Ken Reece.

Whilst every effort has been made to ensure that that the contents
of this publication are accurate, the author cannot accept
responsibility for errors or omissions, or for changes in details
given. The information contained within this publication
is intended only as a general guide.

Walking in the countryside is not without risk of injury or even
fatality. It is the responsibility of the reader to ensure that they,
and anyone accompanying them, are fit to undertake the walk,
are suitably clothed and equipped and take account of the terrain
and the weather conditions. Furthermore, walkers should carry
maps and other navigational aids and have the skills to use these.
Therefore, the author and the publisher will not accept liability for
loss or damage of any nature including damage to property,
injury or death arising to persons directly or indirectly from
information published in this book.

Typeset and cover designed by
www.chandlerbookdesign.com

Cover photograph Hiker on Kinder Scout

A catalogue record for this book is available from
the British Library.

ISBN: 978-1-7397756-0-5

This book contains mapping licensed from the Ordnance Survey with
the permission of the Controller of Her Majesty's Stationery Office.
© Crown Copyright 2021 all rights reserved Licence number 100065069

Printed in Great Britain

This book is dedicated to my brilliant family. Firstly, to my wonderful wife who has supported and encouraged me on my long-distance walks, and with whom I have enjoyed many walks in the countryside and on coastal paths. Also, to my sons and my daughter, with whom I have enjoyed many walks over the years, including several long-distance walks. The quality time I have enjoyed with them on all the many walks, and the friendship and pleasure of walking together that we have shared, is immeasurable.

And finally in memory of our amazing dog, Rocky, who walked with us on many walks and who never tired of walking, not even on the very long and challenging ones.

CONTENTS

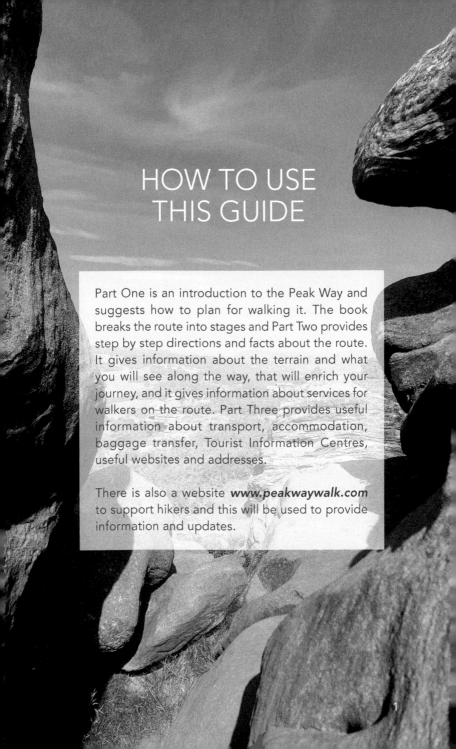

HOW TO USE
THIS GUIDE

Part One is an introduction to the Peak Way and suggests how to plan for walking it. The book breaks the route into stages and Part Two provides step by step directions and facts about the route. It gives information about the terrain and what you will see along the way, that will enrich your journey, and it gives information about services for walkers on the route. Part Three provides useful information about transport, accommodation, baggage transfer, Tourist Information Centres, useful websites and addresses.

There is also a website **www.peakwaywalk.com** to support hikers and this will be used to provide information and updates.

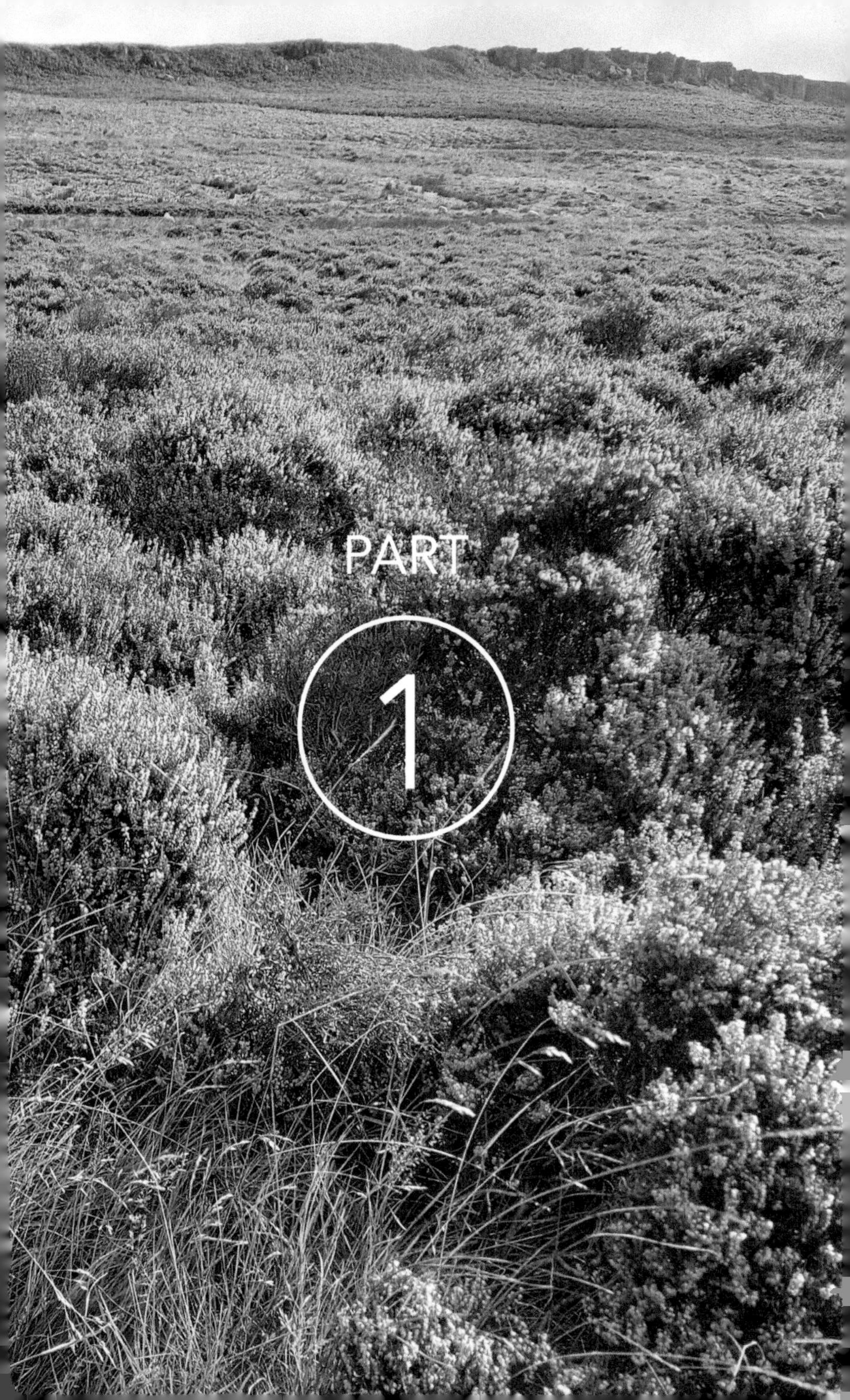

PART 1

INTRODUCTION

You can now explore 155 miles of beautiful countryside, mainly in the Peak District's stunning landscape, on this NEW Long Distance Walking Trail. The walk starts and finishes in Stockport which is just a few miles outside the Peak District National Park. Stockport has local, national and international links and this is a huge benefit for walkers from throughout the UK and overseas. It is also a massive benefit to the Peak District environment, because you can easily reach the start by using public transport but, even if you arrive by car, you will not need to take it into the Peak District. The route has been carefully planned to include many of the best views in the Peak District and features gritstone edges, ridges, dales, many historical features, picturesque villages and passing country pubs and unique cafes. Another great advantage is that there is a range of accommodation at, or close to, the start and finish points for each stage.

The concept

I looked through our bedroom window at the snow-covered Kinder Scout, the highest point in the Peak District. It is just 10 miles or so away, and I longed to be walking there. It is a place I have walked many times before with my walking partner, my family, our dog Rocky and, sometimes, alone, but now I could not. It was January 2021 and the restrictions imposed due to the global Covid-19 pandemic only allowed me to walk locally.

So, I started to walk more frequently on local walks and I was struck by how beautiful the local countryside is, and how lucky I am to live in an urban area that is just literally a few hundred metres from the woodland along the River Goyt. I may have taken it for granted before, but now, being far more mindful, I began to really appreciate just what it offered in terms of the lovely views across beautiful countryside and the great variety of bird, animal, tree and wild flower species that inhabit the area.

Then I started to think about walking from home to Hayfield which is a popular start point for walks on Kinder Scout. So, I took my OS map and started planning what I thought would be the most interesting route, based on my knowledge of this area.

I have been a keen walker for over 40 years now and most of this has been in the Peak District. In addition to the thousands of day-walks I have enjoyed, I have completed several of the UK's long-distance walks; the last one I did was also the longest - the 630-mile South West Coast Path.

So, I developed the idea and started to plan a long-distance route from my home town of Stockport into and around the Peak District. Based on my knowledge of walking in the Peak District, and of my experience of walking long distance trails, I started to create a walking trail that would offer some of the most spectacular views and showcase some of the most interesting heritage in the stunning Peak District, whilst offering accommodation nearby at the end of each day. The Peak Way was born.

Although Stockport is just a few miles outside the Peak District it is an ideal place from which to start and finish a long-distance trail. It has some of the best transport links, being well connected to main rail networks with frequent services and, of course it is on the national motorway network too. It is also well serviced by public transport provided by private bus companies and is located only seven miles from Manchester Airport.

About the Peak District

Opened as the UK's first national park in 1951, the Peak District comprises 555 square miles situated, predominantly in Derbyshire, but also in parts of Cheshire, Staffordshire, Yorkshire and Greater Manchester. The diverse landscape includes extensive moorland, limestone dales, woodland, fields, rivers, reservoirs, caverns and former railway routes. And because of its diversity, it hosts a wide range of wildlife including animals and birds and rare plants and flowers. Although much of its upland is over 1000 ft (300 m), its highest point is Kinder Scout at 2,087 ft (636 m) and much of its landscape comprises gritstone edges and hills.

Route Overview

This new hiking trail is a walk of contrasts. Starting in Stockport, just a few miles outside the Peak District National Park, you will immediately find yourself in lovely countryside. You will soon be in the area known as the Dark Peak which is the higher and wilder part of the Peak District characterised by vast areas of rugged heather moorland, populated with dark gritstone. The views of the surrounding landscape are stunning. Then you will walk in the White Peak which is known for its gently rolling limestone plateau, divided by limestone dales which are often steep-sided, whilst in other places the dales are shallower. You will find clear limestone rivers and streams and colourful hay meadows nestled between dry stone walls. Then there are the picturesque villages and quaint hamlets. You will find that walking in the White Peak is very different than that of the Dark Peak, but equally stunning for its sheer beauty.

Planning the Walk
WALK IT YOUR WAY

This Guide Book shows the Peak Way in stages and each one represents a walk that can be easily walked in a day by most experienced hikers; the table shown on page 9 should be helpful. So, if you have a good level of fitness you can walk the whole trail in two weeks or less. Some of you will want to walk it in a shorter time, whilst some of you may wish to take your time and, possibly build in a rest day or two. Or perhaps you want to take some time to visit the tourist attractions in certain areas.

At the end of Part Two, I have also included an alternative route from Hayfield to Edale in the event that you want to avoid Kinder Scout because of bad weather.

It is advisable to factor in time to have breakfast and pack your kit each morning, to take time for photographs and refreshment stops and time to simply stand and enjoy the views. At the end of each day, you might have to walk, or travel using transport, to your accommodation. Then you will probably need time to unpack, shower and change before you go for your evening meal.

You might decide to split the walk by doing half in one year and the other half in the following year. Whichever way you choose, deciding how you will undertake it is the first step so that you can think about planning your accommodation and travel arrangements.

So, however you decide to walk the Peak Way please do enjoy it.

ROUTE PLANNING GUIDE

Stage	From	To	Miles	Km	Ascent (FEET)	Ascent (METRES)	Page
1	Stockport	Hayfield	14.0	22.6	1,122	342	19
2	Hayfield	Edale	9.9	16.0	2,347	715	29
3	Edale	Hope	8.9	14.3	1,892	577	39
4	Hope	Bamford	16.2	26.0	3,251	991	47
5	Bamford	Grindleford	11.7	18.8	1,958	597	57
6	Grindleford	Bakewell	9.4	15.1	1,556	474	63
7	Bakewell	Matlock	10.0	16.1	810	247	71
8	Matlock	Ashbourne	15.6	25.1	2,506	764	77
9	Ashbourne	Hartington	11.7	18.8	1,505	459	87
10	Hartington	Ashford-in-the- Water	10.0	16.1	978	298	95
11	Ashford-in-the- Water	Buxton	14.5	23.3	2,675	815	103
12	Buxton	Whaley Bridge	8.6	13.9	1,227	374	113
13	Whaley Bridge	Stockport	14.0	22.5	1,411	430	121
Totals			**154.5**	**248.6**	**23,238**	**7083**	

ALTERNATIVE ROUTE FOR STAGE 2

ALT	Hayfield	Edale	6.5	10.5	1,618	493	131

Route Finding

The Peak Way is a new long-distance route and there are no signposts. Using this Guide Book, you should easily be able to follow most of the route because it provides detailed guidance and many of the paths are well defined and obvious. However, there are situations where there are several paths to choose from, or where there is no visible path. Also, particularly in the Dark Peak area, mist can quickly descend and it can be necessary to use a map and compass, or GPS device, to ensure that you walk in the right direction and follow the right path.

MAPS AND APPS

The maps in this Guide Book, used in conjunction with the detailed route description, should help you to stay on track. However, they are not a replacement for a paper map or an app. and it is always advisable to take maps and compass and to know how to use them. Ordnance Survey maps OS Explorer range are recommended because of the 1:25 000 scale which means that they are easy to read and they contain a large amount of detail. Ordnance Survey offers the standard and waterproof versions; Explorer OL1 for the Dark Peak area and Explorer OL24 for the White Peak area. Both of these maps include a mobile download which means that you can download them to your mobile smartphone or tablet. There are also various, relatively inexpensive, apps that you can buy online to download. These apps and the OS downloads mentioned above, will show your current position using your GPS enabled device, and so can be very useful if you do stray off the path, or if you want to check your location on the path. However, if the device fails or the battery power is exhausted, or if it is raining and you are unable to use it, this is when you might need to use map and compass.

You may decide not to buy the OS Explorer 277 map because it only covers the walk from Stockport to Marple (the directions provided in this Guide Book should be adequate) and similarly OS Explorer 259 which only covers a limited area of the walk in the Ashbourne locality and so it might be worth borrowing a library copy.

Fitness and Ability

If you are an experienced hiker then this walk should be well within your capabilities. However, if you think that walking 155 miles is a daunting prospect it would be a good idea to do some training because it does require a certain level of endurance. If you are not a seasoned hiker and you want to train for walking the Peak Way, then it is best to start small and build up your fitness gradually. It would be advisable to include hill walking as part of your training and also carry a rucksack that will have similar weight to the pack that you would carry on the Peak Way.

WHAT TO PACK

Packing your rucksack for walking the Peak Way requires a little thought to keep it as light as possible, but at the same time, packed with essentials that you might need during the walk. There are kit lists online to help you decide, but ultimately it is your decision what to take. Clearly you will also need extra clothing and toiletries for your evenings which you can carry in your rucksack. However, it is well worth considering using the baggage service (see details in Part Three) which will mean that your rucksack is lighter and will ensure that your non-walking clothes and accessories are dry when you arrive at your accommodation.

Getting to Stockport

Stockport is an ideal place from which to start a long-distance trail because of the excellent transport links, being well connected to main rail networks with frequent services to London, Manchester, Liverpool, Birmingham and many other places. It is also well serviced by public transport provided by private bus companies, is on the motorway network and is located only seven miles from Manchester Airport.

ARRIVING BY TRAIN

Stockport is mainly served by Northern and Avanti West Coast trains. Avanti West Coast trains run from Manchester Piccadilly to Stockport and from London Euston to Stockport, whilst Northern Rail connect Buxton to Stockport and Chester to Stockport. In addition to the local rail network, the national rail networks to Manchester and Birmingham, which connect to Stockport, means that you can easily travel by rail from anywhere in England, Scotland and Wales.

www.nationalrail.co.uk

www.thetrainline.com

www.avantiwestcoast.co.uk

www.northernrailway.co.uk

ARRIVING BY COACH

National Express Coaches operate a national service to Manchester and many of the coaches stop at Stockport.

www.nationalexpress.com

ARRIVING BY BUS

There is an extensive network of bus routes throughout the Stockport Borough and beyond and a frequent service to Manchester.

www.tfgm.com

www.stagecoachbus.com

ARRIVING BY AIR

Manchester Airport, just 7 miles from Stockport, is a major international airport which has global routes from many countries as well as regional routes in the UK. There is a direct bus service from the airport to Stockport as well as taxi services.

www.manchesterairport.co.uk

ARRIVING BY CAR

Stockport is ideally located on the M60 and so travel on the national motorway network is easy.

www.theaa.com/routeplanner

www.rac.co.uk/routeplanner

GETTING
TO
THE START

Although there are buses that stop at Woodbank Memorial Park (the start of the Peak Way), I advise you to walk there from the railway station or from Stockport town centre. It is just about one mile from these locations and there are interesting points of interest in this one-mile stretch.

On reaching the main A6 road, head uphill towards Hazel Grove, passing Stockport Town Hall on your left. At the junction, turn left into Edward Street, shortly passing Fred Perry House (named after Stockport tennis legend, Fred Perry, who won the men's singles at Wimbledon in 1934, 1935 and 1936 and was the last Englishman to win the title).

At the junction with Hillgate, walk straight ahead onto Waterloo Road. Almost immediately on the left is the building which was formerly the home of Strawberry Recording Studios which was set up by the band 10cc. From 1968 to 1993, many famous bands and artists recorded their music here including 10cc, Neil Sedaka, The Bay City Rollers, The Buzzcocks, Barclay James Harvest, the Syd Lawrence Orchestra, Paul McCartney, Simply Red, Joy Division, The Smiths, The Stone Roses and many others. You will notice the blue plaque on the building which lists some of the legendary bands and artists who recorded there.

A little further downhill, just past the junction with Hopes Carr, you will see the memorial plaque commemorating the 1967 Stockport air disaster in which 72 passengers and crew were killed and 12 survived. An aircraft full of holiday makers, travelling from Palma de Mallorca to Manchester Airport, crashed in the small open area at Hopes Carr that you can see from here, marking one of the darkest days in Stockport's history. It was amazing that Captain Harry Marlow was able to land the Argonaut airliner in such a small space near the town centre without hitting any major buildings, and without anyone on the ground being killed or injured. Shortly after impact, police officers and members of the public risked their own lives to save 12 people from the wreckage, but then sadly could do no more when the flames engulfed the aircraft and the remaining survivors were killed. The tragedy will never be forgotten by those of us who lived or worked in Stockport at that time.

Continue to the top of Waterloo Road and then turn right onto Spring Gardens, cross the road and cross the main road (St. Mary's Way). From here, walk behind the garage (passing the headquarters of the Peak & Northern Footpaths Society which seems appropriate) and on to Turncroft Lane. Then shortly pass the junction with New Zealand Road until you

reach the corner of the road at the top of the hill. Just ahead of you is the Woodbank Memorial Park which is the start of the Peak Way.

Vernon Park

The adjacent Vernon Park, is Stockport' s oldest park opened in 1858. It was built by Stockport Corporation on land donated by Lord Vernon (George John Warren) on land known as Stringer's Fields, 'for the purpose of public walks and as a place for outdoor exercise'. During 1860 the American Civil War decimated the English cotton trade and Stockport's unemployed mill workers were given low paid work helping to construct some of the park's features. They were so hungry that they gave it the nickname 'Pinch Belly Park'. After decades of neglect, the park was restored back to its Victorian and Edwardian design in 2000.

As it is just a few hundred metres from the start of the Peak Way, you might like to start with light refreshments, or stock up with provisions, at Vernon Park Café. Outside on the terrace you will have extensive views to Pear Mill and way beyond, and you will see two canons that are replicas of the original Russian guns captured at Sevastopol, which were taken and used as scrap during the Second World War.

Woodbank Memorial Park

The entrance of Woodbank Memorial Park is where the Peak Way starts. In 1921 Sir Thomas Rowbotham presented the land to the town, for the purpose of becoming a public park known as Woodbank Memorial Park in honour of the Stockport men who died in the First World War.

The Park is very popular for leisure activities and is also home to Stockport Harriers Athletics Club, which manages the athletics stadium. It has hosted many major leisure events including Stockport Carnivals, the former Stockport Marathons and rock concerts.

PART

2

Peak Forest Canal

STOCKPORT
—— TO ——
HAYFIELD

START	Stockport *(Woodbank Memorial Park)*
FINISH	Hayfield
DISTANCE	14 Miles (22.6Km)
ASCENT	1,122 ft. (342m)
MAPS	OS Explorer 277 & OS Explorer OL1
TERRAIN	The route includes footpaths, tracks, canal towpaths, a short distance on minor roads and a former railway track
REFRESHMENTS	Food and drink are available in Stockport, Marple and New Mills where there are numerous cafes, pubs and restaurants and shops selling food and drink

Pass the main entrance into **Woodbank Memorial Park**, walk down the main drive and follow it round to the right at the bottom, then take the first path (by the signpost for Pear Mill & Alan Newton Way) down between trees until you reach the bottom.

© Crown copyright and database rights 2021 OS 100065069

Walk onto the field ahead and follow the path along the right-hand edge, then down between the trees and cross the bridge ahead over the River Goyt. The **River Goyt** starts its 30 mile journey from its source high on the Peak District moors to eventually join the River Tame at Stockport, forming the River Mersey.

Pear Mill alongside River Goyt

If you look left at this point the top of Pear Mill water tower and chimney will come into view.

Pear Mill, an Edwardian mill built by the River Goyt in 1912, was one of the last cotton-spinning mills to be built, commencing production in 1913. It had 137,312 mule spindles which remained until the 1950s when they were replaced by 33,636 ring spindles, the mill being electrified at the same time. It ceased operation as a textile mill in 1978 and it now houses a mix of retail and leisure facilities.

Once over the bridge turn right on the track passing the electricity pylons and following the path onto a football field. Keeping to the right-hand edge, you will shortly meet a road where you turn right and then straight on along the Alan Newton Way (a cycle route named after former Olympic cyclist, Alan Newton who was born and lived in Stockport).

Follow the track round to the farm, passing in front of the farmhouse to the left and back onto the track shortly passing the historic Goyt Hall Farm (dating back to around 1520) and continuing along the bridleway.

Goyt Hall Farm

Continue, passing the farm on your left and Chadkirk Kennels on your right, until you reach the **Stockport Hydro** which is a community owned hydro-electric scheme. Its two Archimedean screws harness the power of the river to make electricity that is fed into the National Grid. Opened in 2012, it generates enough clean, green energy to power about 60 homes, saving over 100 tonnes of CO_2 per year.

Chadkirk Chapel

Turn left at the main road and cross at the pedestrian crossing into Vale Road. At the bottom of this road there are several signposts and a junction of paths and our route follows the road round to the left (you can use the adjacent footpath), where you will shortly arrive at **Chadkirk Chapel**.

It is a restored 18th Century chapel which has an association through legend with the 7th century missionary St Chad. The Chapel's quiet beauty was enhanced in 1995 by extensive restoration. This included the installation of a specially commissioned life-size statue of St Chad near the altar. It also included the colourful carved wooden panels depicting scenes from the life of the Saint.

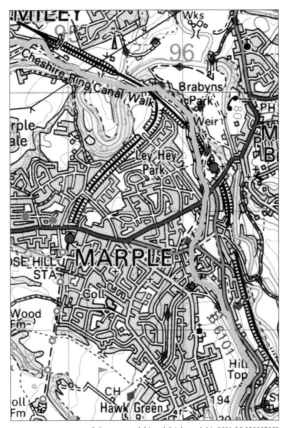

© Crown copyright and database rights 2021 OS 100065069

Follow the road uphill, passing Kirkwood Cottage on your right, and shortly you will reach the sign indicating Peak Forest Canal; turn right up the stone steps and then right on the towpath. The Canal runs for 15 miles between Ashton-under-Lyne, east of Manchester, and Whaley Bridge, Derbyshire. It was authorised by Act of Parliament in 1794 and its purpose was to provide an outlet for the vast limestone deposits around Dove Holes near Buxton. You will soon reach Hyde Bank Tunnel which is 308 yards long and it has no towpath but boats can pass inside it. Boats were propelled through it by 'legging'.

If a boat was being operated single-handedly, then the boatman would lie on his back on top of the cabin and 'walk' along the tunnel roof. If two crew members were available, they would place a plank across the boat, lie on that, back-to-back, and then they would 'walk' along the tunnel sides. Meanwhile, the horse found its own way over the top of the tunnel, a distance of about a half mile.

Follow the path under the road bridge passing Hyde Bank Farm, a wedding and function venue, then turn right into Hydebank lane to shortly meet the path down to the right which will bring you back on the towpath. In less than a mile, you will cross Marple Aqueduct.

Marple Aqueduct and Marple Viaduct

Opened in 1800, it was built to carry the lower level of the Peak Forest Canal across the River Goyt and is the highest canal aqueduct in England at 309 feet long and 100 feet high. Due to lack of maintenance and repair in the decades following its construction, part of it collapsed in 1961 because of frost damage but was restored and re-opened in 1974.

The adjacent **Marple Viaduct** was built by the MS&LR in 1863, to carry the Marple, New Mills and Hayfield Railway that serves Marple Station.

From here, follow the left fork by Aqueduct House to continue along the towpath and soon you will arrive at the lower lock which is one of the 16 locks at Marple, one of the steepest flights in Britain. Although the Peak Forest Canal had been opened for some years at the end of the 18th century, the construction of the locks was not completed until 1805 and a tramway linked the two sections.

When you reach the main road turn right over the road bridge, cross the road and continue along the towpath alongside lock number 9 and then when you reach the next main road, continue on the towpath through the underpass. Just after lock 16 walk over the bridge and turn left onto the towpath and you will shortly reach a bridge which you should walk over and immediately left to re-join the towpath. Continue past the Turf Lea lift bridge and further on past the Higgins Clough swing bridge.

Peak Forest Canal

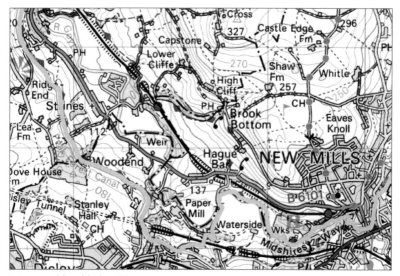

© Crown copyright and database rights 2021 OS 100065069

When you reach bridge 26, leave the towpath and turn left on the lane, under the railway, to meet a junction where you turn right. Continue to follow the road round and shortly after you come alongside the river you will see a sign for the Torrs Riverside Park. Turn right and follow the sign indicating Torrs Millennium Walkway. You will see various paths and you should keep to the right alongside the river and following the sign Mousley Bottom Nature Reserve. Pass between buildings, cross the road onto the path and turn right. Follow the sign Goyt Way via Millennium Way and follow the path down alongside the river on your right. Pass the metal bridge and walk straight onto the magnificent Millennium Way with Torr Vale Mill across the river.

Completed in 1999, the 160-metre long **Millennium Walkway** enabled the Torrs Gorge to be passable for walkers and provides a route through the previously impassable gritstone gorge at Torrs, New Mills which is an area of exceptional natural beauty and unique industrial archaeological heritage.

Millennium Walkway – Torrs Riverside Park

Keep to the left path following the sign for **The Torrs** which is where the Rivers Sett and Goyt come together and where their power was harnessed for over 200 years by mills. The area has mill ruins, weirs, cobbled tracks and archways of bridges towering dramatically overhead and it is well worth spending some time to look around and read the information boards and plaques which tell you about the industrial history, the wildlife and the Hydro Scheme.

Torrs Riverside Park

Above here is **New Mills** a town which was first noted for coal mining, then for cotton spinning, bleaching and calico printing and is home to sweet manufacturer Swizzels Matlow.

Keep left alongside the rockface and, at the signpost, follow Sett Valley Trail and Town Centre. Keep left and over Torr Top Bridge, then continue up the steps and turn right onto **Sett Valley Trail**. The Trail is a 2.5 mile recreational trail for walkers, cyclists and horse riders which runs along the lower valley of the River Sett and follows the trackbed of a former branch railway line from New Mills Central to Hayfield. Follow the Trail to Hayfield, passing through gates and over minor roads and ignoring the other footpaths and bridleways that connect to it. Shortly after passing Birch Vale reservoir, you cross the car park and cross the main road at the pedestrian crossing to emerge in Hayfield alongside St. Matthew's Church.

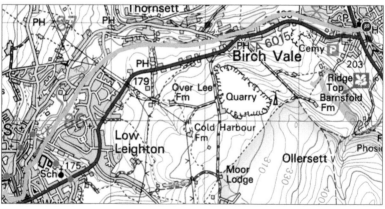

© Crown copyright and database rights 2021 OS 100065069

HAYFIELD
— TO —
EDALE

VIA KINDER SCOUT

START	Hayfield
FINISH	Edale
DISTANCE	9.9 Miles (16Km)
ASCENT	2,347ft. (715m)
MAP	OS Explorer OL1
TERRAIN	The walk includes a steep climb up to Kinder plateau, then walking on rough moorland paths which include stony paths. The final part of the walk is through fields.
REFRESHMENTS	Food and drink are available in Hayfield where there are cafes, pubs and restaurants and shops selling food and drink. No refreshments then until arrival at Edale.

This section of the Trail is over **Kinder Scout**, a moorland plateau in the Dark Peak which, at 636 metres (2,087 ft) above sea level, is the highest point in the Peak District. It is a wild place comprising moorland with strange rock formations (some of which are named), peat bogs and stunning views.

As it is so exposed, the weather can change very quickly and navigation can be difficult, so it is advisable only to walk this section if the weather forecast is favourable. Kinder plateau can be disorientating if you do not know the paths well and it is easy to lose your way, especially if there is low cloud or mist. If the weather is bad on the day that you intend to walk this section of the Peak Way you can, if you wish, choose to take the alternative route from Hayfield to Edale (see page 131).

Hayfield, located at the foot of the Kinder Scout, became a mill village from the 17th century onwards. It is the birth place and childhood home of Arthur Lowe (Captain Mainwaring in the Classic 'Dad's Army') whose home is marked by a blue plaque.

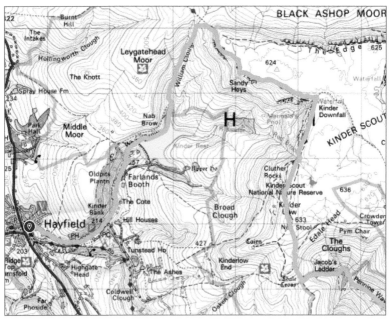

© Crown copyright and database rights 2021 OS 100065069

From the church in Hayfield look for the sign indicating "one mile to the campsite" (Bank Street) and follow this to join Kinder Road. Look for the house on the left which has a blue plaque showing where actor, Arthur Lowe was born. Continue for almost one mile, passing the Sportsman Inn, before arriving at Bowden Bridge car park where you can see another plaque which proclaims "The mass trespass onto Kinder Scout started from this quarry 24th April 1932".

The Kinder Trespass was an organised protest, led by Benny Rothman, involving groups of several hundred walkers who approached Kinder Scout from different directions at the same time. The trespassers who began at Bowden Bridge quarry walked up William Clough to the plateau of Kinder Scout, where there were violent scuffles with gamekeepers. Six ramblers were arrested and detained before being tried by Derby Assizes. Trespass was not a criminal offence at the time, but jail sentences of two to six months were handed out for offences relating to violence against the gamekeepers. It is now accepted that the Mass Trespass helped to bring about the Act of Parliament which established the National Parks and Access to the Countryside. So, as you walk along this next section of the Trail, in the footsteps of these brave historic campaigners, you might want to express your gratitude for their achievement which allows you to walk on this path today, and indeed much of the rest of the countryside.

Continue along Kinder Road for a half mile then turn right over the bridge, following the path/track by the stream then shortly bear left to reach a gate which you pass through and ascend the steep cobbled path to soon reach Kinder Reservoir and a view of the edge of Kinder plateau.

> **KINDER RESERVOIR** took nine years to build and was completed in 1911 to supply water to the Stockport area. It is fed by the River Kinder flowing down William Clough from the upland plateau of Kinder Scout. It has a capacity of over 510 million gallons and covers 44 acres. At the time of its construction, it was claimed to have the largest earth dam in the world.

At the Northern end of the reservoir take the path left of the wooden bridge following the sign for William Clough to ascend gradually up, crossing the stream several times as you continue. Eventually, near the top you walk up rough stone steps and onto a broad track then bear right along the flagged path. The Pennine Way path joins from the left. Continue walking steeply uphill on the flagged path onto the plateau of Kinder Scout. The path ahead (which follows the Pennine Way) is clear.

Start of the walk up William Clough

The lower part of William Clough

Over the years there has been many aircraft crashes in the Peak District and several of these were on Kinder Scout and nearby Bleaklow. Wreckage from one of these lies to the left of the path here, although most of the wreckage lies some distance from the path on Ashop Moor.

> Two Sabre aircraft of No. 66 Squadron crashed in1954 on Ashop Moor. It seems that the aircraft collided in cloud or flew into the side of Kinder Scout and the wreckage was scattered over a wide area. Apparently, due to poor weather, the aircraft were not found for three days.

View from Kinder Scout

Continue walking South East along the perimeter path and eventually you will arrive at Sandy Heys where you will enjoy fine views over Kinder Reservoir before arriving at Kinder Downfall. On the rocks at Sandy Heys, you might notice the initials "GK" which are the initials of George King who founded the Aetherius Society in 1955. Dr. King visited this location which he considered to be a holy mountain charged with spiritual energies.

Below Sandy Heys, is the Mermaid's Pool which, according to legend, is inhabited by a beautiful mermaid who can be seen if you look into the water at sunrise on Easter Sunday.

View from Kinder Downfall

The path continues to **Kinder Downfall** which is the tallest waterfall in the Peak District at 30 metres high and falls dramatically over gritstone cliffs and, during windy conditions, the water spray is blown back on itself and can be seen from miles away. In summer, the river sometimes provides no more than a trickle, whilst in winter months ice forms and climbers can be seen practicing their skills on the enormous ice formation.

Hiker looking towards Kinder Reservoir

Cross the River Kinder here and bear right, heading in a broadly Southerly direction. When you reach a large cairn, bear left climbing slightly and passing a second cairn to reach the trig point at Kinder Low. Several routes lead away from here so you should take care with navigation. From here, head South on the flagged path to pass just left of Edale Rocks (a large block of Millstone Grit) and continue ahead. Shortly, the path bears left and you will reach the top of the Jacobs Ladder path.

> ***JACOBS LADDER*** was named after Jacob Marshall who lived at Edale Head Farm, the ruins of which are just up from the bridge along a track heading west. Jacob was a bragger which was a name given to a pedlar and he took wool to Stockport and traded it for other goods. Because the climb up to Edale Cross was long and stony he cut steps in the hillside and took a shortened route whilst his packhorse ponies followed the longer and winding lane.

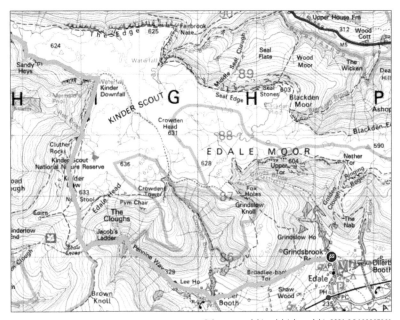

© Crown copyright and database rights 2021 OS 100065069

You will reach a sign "Public Footpath by Jacob's ladder" by a large stone cairn with a great view down the Edale Valley. At the bottom of Jacob's Ladder cross the stone bridge and pass through the wooden gate. The track ahead is obvious, passing several stiles and gates and through the farm to the end where you cross the stone bridge at Upper Booth. Turn left into the farmyard passing a wooden gate with a footpath sign and following the Pennine Way ("Footpath to Edale"). Follow the track passing through several gates and stiles. Rushup Edge and the Great Ridge are on the opposite side of the Valley. The path eventually reaches a track with a signpost. Walk through the gate and turn right on the path and follow it alongside the stream to shortly reach Grindsbrook Booth (known as Edale).

The Great Ridge

EDALE
— TO —
HOPE

VIA THE GREAT RIDGE

START	Edale
FINISH	Hope
DISTANCE	8.9 miles (14.3Km)
ASCENT	1,892 ft. (577m)
MAP	OS Explorer OL1
TERRAIN	The first part of the walk is through fields, followed by a climb up to the moorland on Rushup Edge. The path along the ridge is clearly defined and the descent is through fields.
REFRESHMENTS	Food and drink are available at a café, a pub and a shop in Edale. There are no refreshments then until arrival at Hope.

This section of the walk is mainly along what is known as The Great Ridge, a very popular ridge walk, having stunning views of the Vale of Edale across to Kinder Scout and the striking Winnats Pass winding down to Castleton in the Hope Valley.

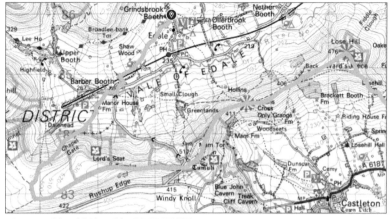

© Crown copyright and database rights 2021 OS 100065069

Although **EDALE** is known as a small village, strictly speaking
it comprises several "booths", formerly herdsmen's shelters,
that are now the hamlets of Upper Booth, Barber Booth,
Ollerbrook Booth and Nether Booth located in the valley
below Kinder Scout. Edale is of course, the start of the
Pennine Way long distance path.

Starting from the top end of Edale near the Nag's Head pub,
the walk passes through several fields to Barber Booth. Pass
through the wooden gate and follow the track to the left of
the café next to the General Store. Just before reaching the
barn take the footpath through the wooden gate on the left
and follow the direction of the signpost to the left of the field.
Pass through gates and stiles and follow the path through
several fields following signposts for Barber Booth. When
you reach the corner in the last field the path bears right to
a wooden gate (next to a metal gate). Walk down the track,
and turn left at the bottom over the railway bridge following
it to Barber Booth.

Walk to the main road and then turn right to reach a stone road
bridge which you cross, and then take the road immediately

right signposted Upper Booth. Shortly on your left, cross the stile and you will see Rushup Edge towering above you. Pass through a wooden gate and across the farm track and over a stile with Manor Head Farm on your left. Cross another stile and turn left following the path by the fence. Cross another stile then pass the gate and continue round left and cross another stile. Follow the path up crossing a stile in a stone wall then pass through a gate and turn right up Chapel Gate track. When you reach a point where there is a paved path to the right, continue following the track round to the left until you reach a sign near a stone wall where you turn left.

The Great Ridge

Follow the path over Rushup Edge to a mound (Lords Seat), a bowl barrow dating back to the Bronze Age. At 550m (1804 ft.), this is the highest point on the ridge from where you will have great views of the Edale Valley and the edge of Kinder Scout on your left and the Hope Valley on your right. Follow the path down to Mam Nick, then walk down through the gate to cross the road and walk up the stone steps to the summit of Mam Tor.

> **MAM TOR**, meaning Mother Hill, and also known as the Shivering Mountain, is named because the landslips on its eastern side have caused the formation of smaller hills. It is a popular location for paragliders. The former A625 road, built in 1819, used to run from Chapel-en-le-Frith to Sheffield but was frequently repaired, following the landslips until, in 1979, the road was permanently closed. Mam Tor is located on the remains of an Iron Age fort and the trig point sits on an ancient burial ground which probably dates back to the Bronze Age.

Looking back down Hope Valley

The route ahead is very clear and the next point on the ridge is Hollins Cross where you cross the stile to resume your walk along the ridge. **Hollins Cross** is a route for walkers from Edale to Castleton or vice versa, but was once a traditional route, known as the 'Coffin Road' when coffins from Edale were taken over to Hope Church until Edale Church was built. Next you walk uphill to **Back Tor which** is an impressive sight rising ahead of you with its steep face dropping sharply down toward the valley. Then at the end of the Great Ridge is **Lose Hill** which marks the descent to your destination at Hope.

Follow the path round to the right and cross the stile and then almost immediately, cross another stile on your right and turn left. Pass through the metal gate down steps, through the wooden gate then right through a metal gate with Hope village straight ahead. Cross the field to the barn. Cross the wooden footbridge on the left and then cross the next stile by the tree. Pass through several fields to reach "The Meadows", keep straight ahead through two wooden gates then cross the

Hikers on the Great Ridge

railway over the metal bridge. Follow the path through several more gates to a road. Turn right and follow the road round and, just before the medical centre, take the footpath on your right to the main street in Hope.

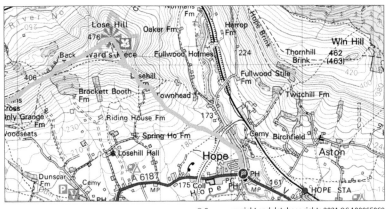

© Crown copyright and database rights 2021 OS 100065069

The Salt Cellar

HOPE
—— TO ——
BAMFORD

START	Hope
FINISH	Bamford
DISTANCE	16.2 miles (26.0Km)
ASCENT	3,251 ft. (991m)
MAP	OS Explorer OL1
TERRAIN	Most of the walk is on high moorland and along gritstone edges above the reservoirs with a section of level walking alongside Derwent Reservoir.
REFRESHMENTS	There is a café and shop in Hope and a refreshment kiosk and toilets at Fairholmes Visitor Centre.

The village of **Hope** is located in the valley at the point where Peakshole Water (which is named after its source the Peak Cavern) flows into the River Noe (which flows from its source, the confluence of two streams running off Kinder Scout).

© Crown copyright and database rights 2021 OS 100065069

Start on Edale Road, opposite the church and shortly turn right into Bowden Lane, signed Hope Cemetery. Walk over the footbridge and straight on down the minor road passing under the railway bridge and bearing left on the road, then keep left following the footpath sign for Hope Cottage and Coach House. Pass through a stile into a field and follow the path ahead. At Fulwood Farm cross the stile by the gate and continue on the track uphill. Pass through a metal gate and take the left-hand fork signed Public Bridleway. Cross a stile

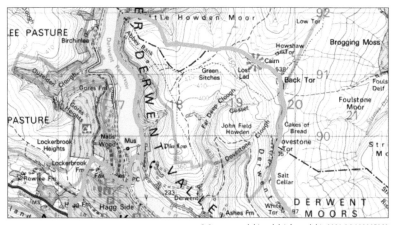

© Crown copyright and database rights 2021 OS 100065069

by a gate and continue until you reach **Hope Cross**, a 7-foot high waymark stone which shows the point where ancient packhorse routes through the Peak District crossed on a former Roman road. Pass through the gate and continue uphill until shortly you reach a stile by a gate where you turn right to follow the sign for Public Bridleway Hagg Farm. Pass through a gate into the forest and downhill on the stony path. At the bottom, just before a wooden gate, bear left and continue on the stony track downhill. At the point where another track joins from the left, turn right over the footbridge, cross the main road at the top and up the minor road signed Hagg Farm Centre. Once a 19th Century hill farm, **Hagg Farm** is now an Outdoor Education Centre that provides a range of outdoor activities and accommodation for groups. Shortly where the road bends left, continue uphill straight ahead on the forest path. Pass through a gate, cross a stile and at the signpost walk straight on following the sign for Lockerbrook and Fairholmes. On reaching the Lockerbrook Outdoor Centre you will get a glimpse of the **Ladybower Reservoir** which was built between 1935 and 1943 to supplement the neighbouring Derwent and Howden reservoirs which supply water to the East Midlands.

PART TWO | Hope to Bamford   49

Ladybower Reservoir

Walk past the Centre to reach a signpost where you turn right through a gate following the path for Fairholmes. Almost immediately reach a gate and bear right onto the path and through another gate into the forest where you continue downhill, crossing two tracks, down to a wooden gate at the road. Cross the road to **Fairholmes Visitor Centre** which offers refreshments and toilet facilities and an information service. This is a good place to stock up on refreshments if you need them because it is the last opportunity before arriving at Bamford.

Follow the sign "To Dams" through a wooded area and onto a road where you will see the huge dam wall. Shortly, at the junction, turn left uphill following the sign for Derwent Dam East Tower. Pass through the gate onto the road and walk alongside Derwent reservoir.

Howden Dam

During WW2, pilots of the 617 Squadron practised their low-level flights, as part of the training for the «Dam Busters» raids, because of its similarity to the German dams.

Derwent Reservoir

After approximately 1.5 miles from Fairholmes, at the sign for Bradfield and Strines, bear right up the path. Almost immediately, ignore the path to the right and walk uphill straight ahead and pass through the wooden gate. At the sign for Little Howden Moor, at the junction of paths, walk uphill on the right-hand path. When you reach a wooden gate on your left, cross the stile just past it to the path on the left, down to small stream. Then almost immediately, look carefully and follow the path on the right uphill. Shortly you will encounter several paths on the moorland here; aim for the hill straight ahead continuing steeply uphill on stone steps. Follow the slabbed path up to the cairn and toposcope at Lost Lad.

The name of the cairn known as **LOST LAD**, derives its name from a legend about a shepherd boy from the former Derwent village which was located in the valley before the Ladybower Reservoir was built. According to the legend, the boy was lost on the moors whilst herding sheep in a winter blizzard and he died of exposure in these harsh conditions. His body was found the following spring by a passing shepherd and nearby were the words "Lost Lad" written on a rock. It is easy to understand how anyone could be lost here in hazardous conditions.

The path to Derwent Edge

The path is obvious now being slabbed for most of the way and passing the various rock formations named on the OS map. Next you will reach Back Tor which is the highest point of the Edge at 1765 feet (538 metres) and then the distinctive Cakes of Bread, named because of its visual appearance, is one of several gritstone tors which you will find as you walk along **Derwent Edge**.

Derwent Edge

After the Cakes of Bread, the path reaches Dovestone Tor, the most significant outcrop on the Derwent Edge, followed by the Salt Cellar, White Tor and Wheel Stones. Eventually you will reach a junction of paths by a sign where you walk straight ahead and pass the Hurkling Stones (rocks) on your left. Descend to Whinstone Lee Tor where, at the next junction of paths, you turn left signed Cutthroat Bridge. The path descends for about one mile to the curiously named **Cutthroat Bridge**, named because a man was found there with his throat cut in l635.

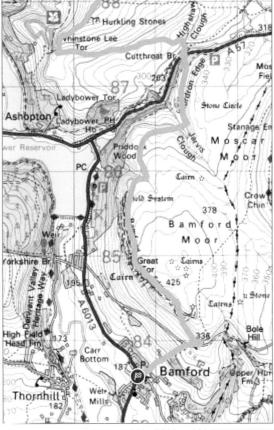

© Crown copyright and database rights 2021 OS 100065069

Ladybower Reservoir from Derwent Edge

Cross the main road and over the stile opposite and walk up the track. Just past a plantation of trees, follow the path on your right down to a stream and then uphill. Follow this path round to reach Pillars (a small rocky outcrop) and continue to follow the path taking a right fork ahead. You will now enjoy great views of Ladybower Reservoir and Win Hill. Descend to a stream and then walk uphill, following the right- hand path at the fork up to **Bamford Edge** which is a gritstone escarpment, being very popular with walkers and climbers, that has superb views of Ladybower Reservoir and the Derwent Valley. Walk to the other end of Bamford Edge, through stones and descend, bearing right at the next fork, to the road. Turn right on the road and then shortly, at the corner, walk left down the track and road down into Bamford.

BAMFORD
—— TO ——
GRINDLEFORD

START	Bamford
FINISH	Grindleford
DISTANCE	11.7 miles (18.8Km)
ASCENT	1,958 ft. (597m)
MAP	OS Explorer OL1
TERRAIN	Most of this walk is on high moorland paths, a path down Padley Gorge and then through fields
REFRESHMENTS	There are no refreshments available until Grindleford

The village of **Bamford**, located alongside the River Derwent, is 11 miles west of Sheffield and 25 miles east of Manchester.

Start the walk by the seating area in the village and retracing your steps from the previous stage to walk up Fidlers Well. Keep straight ahead on Bamford Clough rising steeply to meet New Road at the top. Turn right on the road and cross over the stile by the wooden gate onto Moscar Moor. Bear right and follow the broad grass track which soon follows the right edge of the disused quarry. When you reach the top right-hand corner of the quarry, the path is straight ahead (North) for just over 0.5 mile where it bears right (NNE) for a further 2 miles across featureless moorland. However, it is easy to stray from the path which, in many areas, is not clearly defined. The walk across the moor, approximately 2.5 miles (4Kms.), is typically rough ground and there are also boggy areas. As a point of reference, once you see the end of Stanage Edge, that is where you are aiming to reach, but because of the challenging terrain and difficulty of keeping to the path, it is advisable to use a navigation aid. The use of an app which uses GPS, such as the OS app, would be useful because you should be able to follow the path by knowing your current position whilst walking across the moor. The path eventually rises to meet the clear path where you turn right up to Stanage End and walk along the Stanage Edge path for about 4.25 miles where you walk down to meet the road.

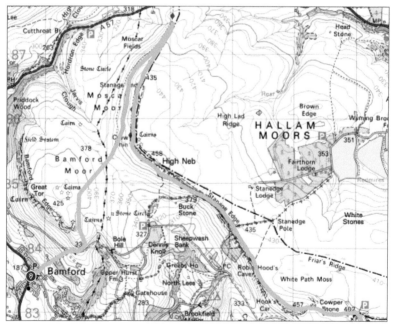

© Crown copyright and database rights 2021 OS 100065069

STANAGE EDGE, a gritstone escarpment, is approximately 4 miles long and is the largest of the gritstone cliffs that overlook Hathersage with extensive stunning views of the Dark Peak moorland and the Hope Valley. Its highest point, High Neb, is 1,503 ft (458m) and the area is very popular with climbers of various abilities who come to tackle the many and varied routes. The area around Hathersage was once a major centre for the quarrying of millstones once used for grinding grain in the mills, and you may see abandoned millstones scattered around.

Stanage Edge

The path on Stanage Edge

© Crown copyright and database rights 2021 OS 100065069

Turn left on the road and walk into the car park on your right just before the road bridge then pass through the metal gate on the left by the footpath sign. Bear right on the path which rises slightly and follow the clear path ahead to Higger Tor. When you reach the top, it is a good idea to find your intended route as there are several paths on Hathersage Moor below.

Padley Gorge

If you walk to the left-hand corner of the summit, you will see the remains of the Carl Wark structure which is thought to have possibly been an Iron age hill fort, although this is uncertain. You should see the path that leads to the Carl Wark remains and this is the path that you want. From the left-hand corner of the Higger Tor summit, look carefully for this path and a short scramble through rocks and down stone steps will take you to it. Follow the path, passing through the Carl Wark ruins and from here continue down to meet the main road at Toad's Mouth. At the road, turn left over the road bridge and then pass through the gate immediately on your right. Shortly at the fork in the path, bear right and cross the footbridge over the stream. At the next footbridge continue straight on, signed Padley Gorge, keeping to the right of the stream all the way to the bottom of the gorge. At the bottom, pass through the gate and walk down the stone road. Turn right at the bottom and along the stone road past Brunt's Barn, cross the cattle grid and then turn immediately left to cross the railway bridge. Continue ahead and, at the waymarker, turn left through a gap in the stone wall and cross the field to another stone wall which you follow round to reach a small gate on the left. Walk through this across the stream then turn right to follow the footpath waymarker. The path follows the riverside through two fields to meet the road where you turn right over the road bridge into Grindleford.

View from Curbar Edge

GRINDLEFORD
—— TO ——
BAKEWELL

START	Grindleford
FINISH	Bakewell
DISTANCE	9.4 miles (15.2Km)
ASCENT	1,556 ft. (474m)
MAP	OS Explorer OL24
TERRAIN	Through woodland, along high-level moorland edges followed by walking through Chatsworth Estate, a rough track and bridleway and minor roads
REFRESHMENTS	Cafes & pubs at Baslow and café and refreshment kiosks at Chatsworth

This stage continues on the high-level escarpments of Froggatt Edge, Curbar Edge and Baslow Edge before dropping to the village of Baslow and passing through the magnificent Chatsworth Estate. If you have sufficient time, it is well worth visiting Chatsworth House and Gardens, before continuing through the picturesque village of Edensor and then on to the destination of Bakewell.

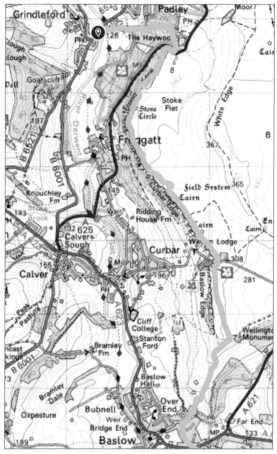

© Crown copyright and database rights 2021 OS 100065069

From Grindleford village, cross the road bridge over the River Derwent and follow the Public Footpath sign opposite Toll Bar Cottage. Walk up the rough track, with the church on your left, and just past a house on your left follow the track round the bend and into woodland. The path rises and when you reach a fork in the paths follow the right-hand path uphill. At the next junction of paths, and the one after that, bear right on the path. Near the top, the path continues right and descends to a stream then uphill to the main road. Pass through the gate, cross the road and pass through the gate on the left. The path ahead is clear and initially passes through woodland before reaching the heather clad moorland on the Froggatt Edge escarpment.

Hikers on Curbar Edge

Froggatt Edge

The Wellington Memorial

The path along Froggatt Edge and its neighbour, Curbar Edge, is obvious and the only deviations you are likely to make are to admire the views from the edge. At the end of Curbar Edge pass through the gate and follow the footpath to your right signed Baslow Edge then cross the road and follow the path opposite. Follow the clear path ahead and eventually you will pass a prominent rock on your left, known as the Eagle Stone. Apparently, it was customary for the young men of Baslow to prove their fitness for marriage by climbing the stone. Just past here you reach the end of the path. If you want to see the Wellington monument, turn left for a short distance and then retrace your steps. Otherwise, turn right on the path down to a gate and pass through.

Curbar Edge

The rough track takes you downhill until you reach Ladywell Farm where it becomes a tarmac road. Continue down, passing houses, until you reach the road at the bottom. Turn left here (Eaton Hill) down to Baslow centre.

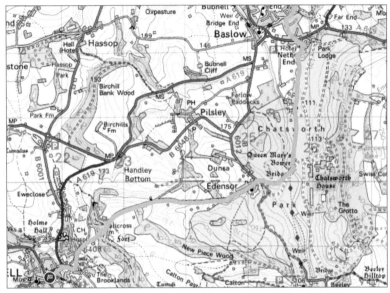

© Crown copyright and database rights 2021 OS 100065069

Cross the main road and the village green opposite the car park and turn left on this road over the river bridge then turn right signed Chatsworth in front of the cottages. Follow the track round to a metal kissing gate and into the Chatsworth Estate then follow the right-hand path. Continue straight ahead at Bar Brook Lodge and you will soon see the magnificent Chatsworth House, with the cricket pitch on your right.

> **CHATSWORTH HOUSE** is a splendid stately home where the Duke and Duchess of Devonshire reside, and which has been passed down through 16 generations of the Cavendish family.

Chatsworth Estate

It sits in the 105-acre garden which is the product of nearly 500 years of careful cultivation and includes an arboretum, rock garden, fountains and sculptures. In the house there are over 25 rooms to explore, including the magnificent Painted Hall, Regal State Rooms, restored Sketch Galleries and beautiful Sculpture Gallery. There are various restaurants and shops across the estate, including the Estate's Farm Shop.

Cross the road bridge over the river and take the path on the right uphill, and St. Peter's Church at Edensor soon comes into view. At the bottom, cross the road into Edensor Village.

> The village of **EDENSOR** has St Peter's Church at its heart, and Edensor Tea Cottage which is a lovely place to stop for afternoon tea or other refreshments. When the 6th Duke and Joseph Paxton rebuilt Edensor, they combined a variety of architectural styles. The result is a picturesque village that is very much at the heart of the Chatsworth community.

Edensor Village

Homemade jams at Edensor

Walk up the road through the village and continue straight ahead uphill on the rough track. At the road, turn left uphill and once over the rise as you walk downhill, just before Ball Cross Farm, take the bridleway on your left steeply downhill through woodland. Cross the golf course, from where you will see Bakewell Church in the distance. Turn left on the road and left again at the junction and walk downhill until you meet the main road at the bottom. Turn left here into Bakewell.

River Derwent at Rowsley

BAKEWELL
—— TO ——
MATLOCK

START	Bakewell
FINISH	Matlock
DISTANCE	10 miles (16.1 Km)
ASCENT	810 ft (247m)
MAP	OS Explorer OL24
TERRAIN	Mainly through woodland and through pastures and fields
REFRESHMENTS	Refreshments are available from the Post Office and pub at Rowsley and the pub at Darley Bridge

Situated on the banks of the River Wye, **Bakewell** is a magnet for Peak District tourists and is well known for its unique and delicious Pudding. You will find several shops where you can indulge yourself and enjoy one of these unique confectionary treats or any of the other delicious pastries on offer.

Bakewell is famous for its unique puddings

River Derwent at Bakewell

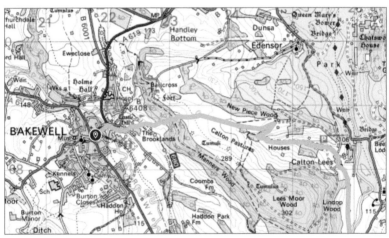
© Crown copyright and database rights 2021 OS 100065069

Leave the centre of Bakewell and walk over the road bridge crossing the river, then turn right into Station Road and then immediately right into Coombs Road. Shortly at The Outrake, turn left up the tarmac track, bearing right at the cottages. Pass through a gate and continue on the path with the stone wall immediately to your right. Shortly cross a stile and through a gate on a stone bridge then follow the path up to emerge on the golf course. Follow the path across (as signed) into the woods and follow the path uphill. At a junction of paths by a small stream bear left continuing uphill. Then at the next junction of paths continue uphill, bearing left. At the top pass through the gate in the stone wall onto Calton Pastures then bear right on a path to pass a plantation of trees on your left. Pass through a gate by the pond and through another gate just past it. The path bears slightly right and then, almost immediately, straight ahead aiming left of the plantation of trees ahead and slightly right. Pass through a gate and follow the path left of the

Well dressing at Rowsley

plantation. The path bears left towards a barn and a house then, at the junction of paths, turn right on the path downhill, pass through a gate and continue downhill, then pass through another gate on a stony track between cottages. Follow the track down to the bottom, pass through a gate then bear right to pass Calton Houses and Cottages, signed Rowsley. After passing the cottages, cross the stone stile (ignore the signpost to Rowsley) and bear left on the path, cross the ladder stile and follow the path right through large fields. Almost at the end of the last field, pass through a wooden gate on your right then through another gate by the river into another field where the path bears right. Then walk along the farm track to pass under a stone bridge to the road at Home Farm. Turn left along the road into Rowsley.

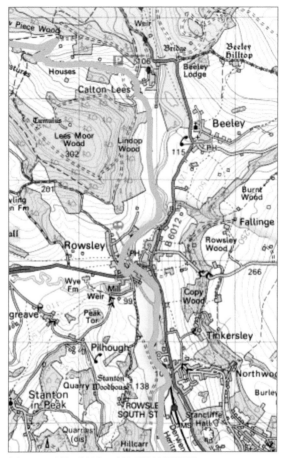

© Crown copyright and database rights 2021 OS 100065069

Turn left on the main road, cross the road bridge over the river and pass the Grouse and Claret pub. Turn right into Old Station Road and then immediately right into the car park, then follow the path in the left-hand corner. At the factory gate bear right on the path signed Derwent Valley Heritage Way (DVHW) alongside the river. When you reach the Peak Railway, follow the path signed Churchtown and walk through the fields to reach Abbey Farm. Pass the school and bear right at the road junction.

Peak Heritage Railway

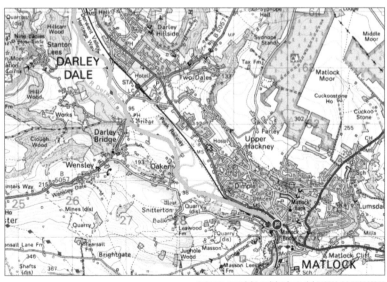

© Crown copyright and database rights 2021 OS 100065069

Just past the church, follow the footpath on your right signed DVHW through fields to the track by the cricket pitch. Turn right at the main road into Darley Bridge, cross the road bridge over the river and turn immediately left into Wenslees. After the cottages pass through a metal gate onto a rough tarmac track to another metal gate and pass through this bearing right uphill on the rough track. Just after the right-hand bend, opposite the bungalow, follow the footpath left signed DVHW and follow the riverside path. Walk down the steps just before the railway and turn right under the railway following the path into Matlock centre.

River Derwent Matlock

MATLOCK
—— TO ——
ASHBOURNE

START	Matlock
FINISH	Ashbourne
DISTANCE	15.6 Miles (25.1Km)
ASCENT	2,506 ft. (764m)
MAPS	OS Explorer OL24 & 259
TERRAIN	This section includes riverside paths, road-side walking, minor roads, a former railway track, fields and alongside a reservoir
REFRESHMENTS	There are cafes and pubs in Matlock, Matlock Bath and Cromford, and light refreshments are available at Middleton Top Information Centre. There is a restaurant, light refreshments and toilets at Carsington Water and a pub at Hognaston.

Located alongside the river Derwent, **Matlock** benefitted from hydrotherapy and cloth mills. It was pioneering industrialist John Smedley who recognised the potential of the thermal water for hydrotherapy in Matlock, and in the 19th Century he developed it as a famous fashionable spa town.

© Crown copyright and database rights 2021 OS 100065069

Start by the road bridge in the centre of Matlock and walk along the riverside footpath in Hall Leys Park, passing the bandstand on your left and walking straight on at the signpost for Pic Tor. At the road, turn right signed Knowleston Gardens/ Pic Tor, cross the wooden bridge and turn right on the path. At the junction of paths, turn left under the bridge signed

High Tor. Follow the path ahead uphill and at the buildings turn sharp right through the gate signed High Tor grounds. Pass two viewing points and continue uphill. Near to the top you will come to a field with good views of Riber Castle on your left. This was John Smedley's house until his death in 1874 and has had various uses including as a zoo and a school. At the junction of paths by the High Tor information board bear left and onto a tarmac path downhill. You may see cable cars between the trees on your right. Watch carefully for a narrow path on your right and take this. The path soon becomes wider down stone steps through woodland. It winds steeply down until you reach the cable car station where you continue straight ahead under the bridge. Cross the bridge over the river and turn left on the main road into **Matlock Bath** which is set in the beautiful gorge of the River Derwent, with attractive riverside gardens, wooded hillsides and rocky limestone crags. Today, it is a tourist destination as it has been since the late 17th Century when the spa waters were discovered, and subsequently its development in the Victorian era.

Cable Cars above Matlock

Opposite the Midland pub on the corner, turn right into Holme Road and, at the top, continue along Upperwood Road. You will soon see the River Derwent and Matlock Bath below on your left and Gulliver's Kingdom Theme Park above on the hillside. The path rises steeply and enters woodland near the top. At the signpost by the Upperwood Bench, bear left on the track between houses. Continue on the path, passing Clifton Cottage and signed Public Footpath to Scarthin and into woodland. Continue downhill and, at a waymarker, walk straight on. Continue downhill to the road and turn left into **Cromford**.

It is arguably best known for its historical connection with Richard Arkwright, and the nearby **CROMFORD MILL** which he built outside the village in 1771. Sir Richard Arkwright built the world's first water powered cotton mills in Cromford where he pioneered the factory system. As you walk through Cromford, you may notice the terraced 3 storey buildings in which the mill workers lived.

Sir Richard Arkwright's Mill at Cromford

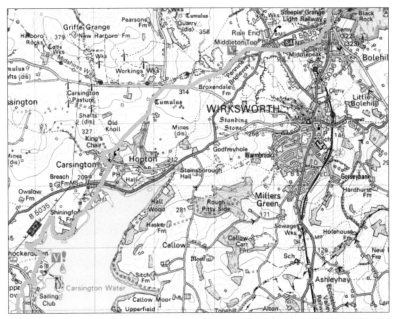

© Crown copyright and database rights 2021 OS 100065069

Walk on the path alongside the road through Cromford uphill until you reach a bridge behind the sign for Wirksworth. Take the path on the right just before the bridge up to **Steeple Grange Light Railway** and cross the lines to pass through the gate onto High Peak Trail and turn right. The 17 mile long trail follows the route of the former High Peak Railway Line, opened in 1831 to transport minerals between Cromford Canal and the Peak Forest Canal. It closed in 1967 since when it has been used as a leisure trail by walkers, cyclists, runners and horse riders.

After a short distance you will walk steeply up to **Middleton Top** where there are good views across the countryside. Inside the building is the restored steam engine, built in 1829, which was used to haul wagons up the Middleton incline.

Middleton Top

Continue, passing through Hopton Tunnel until you reach a signpost and follow for Carsington down to the road and straight across at the crossroad signed Hopton/Carsington. When you reach Dene Farm take the public footpath in the field opposite and follow it diagonally left uphill, then through fields until you reach the top then pass through the stile in the corner by the woods and walk steeply downhill following the waymarker posts. You will see the village of Carsington below and, beyond that, ***Carsington Water***. At the bottom, pass through the wooden gate down steps and between buildings and turn left on the road. At the junction bear right into School Lane and then right into Back Lane and walk straight ahead at the signpost. Continue straight ahead and cross the road, turn right then immediately left and follow the red waymarkers for Carsington Water Circular Route. Follow the perimeter path/ track round the reservoir past the Sports and Leisure Centre and Visitor Centre and continue passing the grassed area and children's play area on your left to resume the perimeter path/ track. The reservoir was opened by the Queen in 1992. It is a popular leisure facility for walkers, cyclists, horse riders, anglers and birdwatchers as well as providing a watersports centre.

Descent into Carsington with Carsington Water in the background

Carsington Water

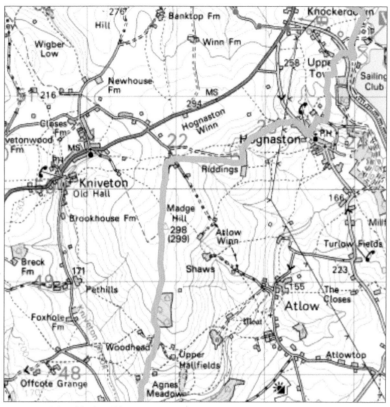

© Crown copyright and database rights 2021 OS 100065069

Shortly, when you reach the Sailing Club, turn right to the main road, cross this and walk to the public footpath sign on the left. Cross the stile and walk along the left-hand side of the field to a wooden gate which you pass through and walk diagonally right. Pass through two wooden gates in a fence and beyond two stone pillars to the next stile. Turn right at the end of the next field and pass through a squeeze stile then turn left on a path between hedges which broadens into a rough track. Cross the stream at the bottom and turn right. At the junction turn left on a tarmac road then turn right on the main road. Walk through the village of Hognaston and turn left at

View from Madge Hill

High Barn to walk between houses. Shortly where another track comes from the right, turn left over a cattle grid along a tarmac road into fields. At the junction of paths by the next cattle grid walk ahead downhill over another cattle grid and follow bearing left to follow the footpath sign. Just before you reach the farmyard turn right up the footpath then, keeping to the hedgerow on the left walk straight ahead to the gate then uphill ahead to the next gate. Then bear left towards the

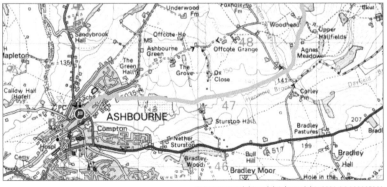

© Crown copyright and database rights 2021 OS 100065069

trees, pass through a metal gate and across a part tarmac track through a wood to a track where you turn left. Continue on this track, through a metal gate, to pass the trig point on Madge Hill from where there are fine views. Walk down the track, through another metal gate then passing the glamping pods site and Woodhead farmhouse. Continue down the road to the junction and turn right at the road junction and immediately take the public footpath on the left over the footbridge. The path now passes through a series of fields for almost 2 miles passing over stiles and through gates, some of which are not easy to find; I therefore advise you to use a map or an app. to ensure that you follow the path through these fields and to avoid straying from the path. Near the end of this path, you will walk through woodland where you continue across a track into fields. Then finally walk onto the rugby pitch where you turn immediately right and then left at the corner behind the houses, to take you to the B5035 road into Ashbourne.

ASHBOURNE
—— TO ——
HARTINGTON

START	Ashbourne
FINISH	Hartington
DISTANCE	11.7 miles (18.8km)
ASCENT	1,505 ft. (459m)
MAP	OS Explorer OL24
TERRAIN	Mainly along riverside paths along deep-sided dales and fields
REFRESHMENTS	Refreshments are available at Ashbourne Cycle Hire (on Tissington Trail), Dovedale car park and Milldale

This stage of the walk follows the River Dove which was fished by Izaak Walton in the 17th Century, who famously wrote The Compleat Angler published in 1653, and his friend Charles Cotton who also contributed to the book. Two hotels are named after them; the Izaak Walton Hotel near Ilam and the Charles Cotton Hotel located in the lovely village of Hartington which is the destination of this stage of the Peak Way.

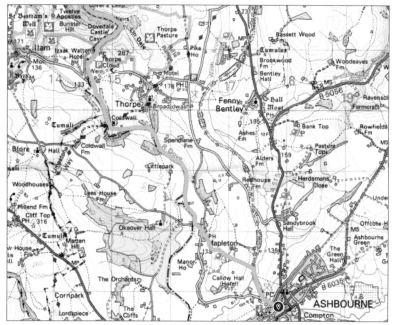

© Crown copyright and database rights 2021 OS 100065069

ASHBOURNE, sometimes known as 'The Gateway to Dovedale' is a market town which has many historical buildings and independently owned shops, cobbled streets and hidden alleyways. The town is famous for the annual Royal Shrovetide Football Match, which has been played since at least 1667, although its origins may date back centuries earlier.

Leave the footpath on Station Road, opposite the Station Hotel, turn right on the track signed Tissington Trail and walk through the tunnel to arrive at the cycle hire centre. Continue on the trail, crossing the river and uphill to a gate and then immediately left down wooden steps. Continue uphill and then between fences by the campsite. Cross the tarmac track following the sign for Mapleton through a gate and then through another gate into the field. Walk downhill to a hedge where there is a junction of paths with small directional arrows and turn right on the path, pass through stiles then bear left to pass through a gate to the road at Mapleton. Turn right and take the path opposite Okeover Arms across the field to the road bridge. Cross the road and through the gate opposite following the riverside footpath, initially by the river then bearing right to a gap in the hedge to re-join the river. Follow the path through fields and across stiles and pass farm outbuildings to reach Coldwell Bridge. Pass through a wooden gate then take the riverside path immediately on the right through fields until you reach the road bridge. Cross the road and continue on the riverside path opposite. Pass Dovedale car park on your left and, at the wooden footbridge, keep straight ahead on the path.

As you enter the steep sided valley of **Dovedale**, you will see Thorpe Cloud (an isolated limestone hill rising to 942 feet), shortly before reaching the stepping stones. This is a popular place with walkers and families, especially at weekends when you will see people queuing to cross them.

The stepping stones at Dovedale

River Dove

Caves at Dovedale

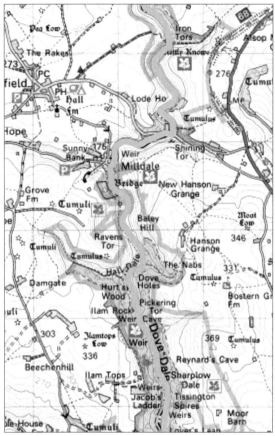

© Crown copyright and database rights 2021 OS 100065069

Pass through the stone stile by the gate following the path signed **Milldale**. Shortly walk up the stone steps to reach a place known as Lovers Leap. Along the path you will see dramatic cliffs and strange limestone formations as well as several caves of various sizes, some of which are named on the OS map. The path continues alongside the River Dove for about 2.5 miles where you cross Viator's Bridge, a former packhorse bridge, into the hamlet of Milldale with its 17th and 18th Century cottages.

At the road junction keep right alongside the river for about 0.5 mile and, at the next road junction, turn right over the bridge and immediately left on the path alongside the river signed Beresford Dale, Wolfscote Dale and Hartington. As you follow the River Dove on its journey, you will enter an idyllic ravine, **Wolfscote Dale**, a rugged steep sided valley with imposing peaks.

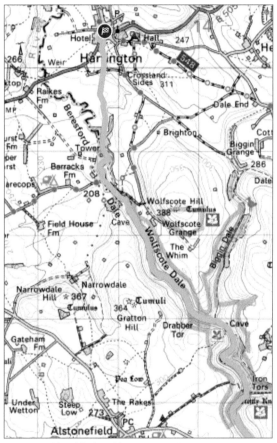

© Crown copyright and database rights 2021 OS 100065069

Footbridge at Beresford Dale

At a signpost by a building keep straight ahead signed Hartington and again at the next signpost follow the path for Hartington. At the end of Wolfscote Dale you will meet a stone wall next to a footbridge; walk straight ahead here and cross a small stream into a field. At the end of the field cross the footbridge and turn right on the path beside the river into Beresford Dale, a beautiful tree lined dale enclosed by limestone cliffs. Shortly cross the river over the footbridge then away from the river into Morson Wood. Pass through the gate in the stone wall and keep on the path ahead through fields until you reach a stone wall where you cross the track and follow the path through fields into Hartington.

Hartington Cheese Shop

Sheldon village

HARTINGTON
— TO —
ASHFORD IN
THE WATER

START	Hartington
FINISH	Ashford in the Water
DISTANCE	10 miles (16.1Km)
ASCENT	978 ft. (298m)
MAP	OS Explorer OL24
TERRAIN	Along minor roads, a former railway track, through villages and fields
REFRESHMENTS	Drinks and food are available at a café, two pubs and a shop in Hartington. Refreshments are available at Hartington signal box (Tissington Trail) and Parsley Hay Cycle Centre. There is a café and pub at Monyash and a pub at Sheldon.

The popular village of **Hartington**, with its stone cottages and houses, used to be known for mining and cheese making. Cheese making in Hartington dates back to the 1870's when Dove Dairy (later called Hartington Cheese Factory) was built. Following its closure in 2009, with the loss of 150 jobs, cheese production re-started by a company called the Hartington

Creamery and a small-scale cheese factory was developed just outside the village of Hartington. You can find a wide range of cheeses, including the local cheeses, in the Hartington Cheese Shop. The market place in Hartington was the first village in Derbyshire to be granted a Market Charter in 1203 and the duck pond was used as drinking water for the animals. Parts of St. Giles Church date back to the 1200's.

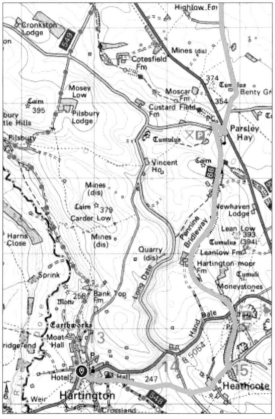

© Crown copyright and database rights 2021 OS 100065069

Hartington Youth Hostel

From the village centre, with the Beresford Tea Rooms on your right, walk up the road and almost immediately turn right into Hall Bank. Continue uphill shortly passing Hartington Youth Hostel, formerly a manor house and one of the most impressive buildings in Hartington. Continue on the road, passing tracks to Biggin, until at the bottom you reach a road junction by a pond. Turn right and then immediately left following the signpost to Heathcote. You will shortly reach this small hamlet and, at the crossroads, continue on the road straight ahead.

After almost 0.25 mile, at the bridge, turn right to access the Tissington Trail then right onto the Trail. The 13-mile long **Tissington Trail** runs from Ashbourne to Parsley Hay and is popular with walkers and cyclists. It was formerly a railway line, opened in 1899, which ran from Buxton to Ashbourne until its closure in 1967. Shortly, you will see the former Hartington signal box (where there are refreshments and toilets).

Heathcote Mere

Hartington Station was one of the busiest on the line and was used for passengers and freight; it served the local quarries to transport limestone. Continue along the trail which, just before reaching Parsley Hay, is joined by the High Peak Trail. Walk on to the cycle hire centre (where there are refreshments and toilets) and then walk along the road to meet the main road. Cross the main road and immediately turn right into the lane signposted Monyash and walk along this roadside, for about 2 miles, to the village of Monyash.

MONYASH was formerly a major lead mining area and was also known for limestone quarrying, marble polishing and farming. During the 19th Century it had many tradespeople including blacksmiths, cobblers, butchers, wheelwrights, wool merchants, joiners, dressmakers, shoe makers, policeman and five pubs. Today, farming and tourism are the prominent industries. St Leonards Church was founded in 1198. You will notice a stone cross on the village green which was the location of the weekly market dating back to 1340.

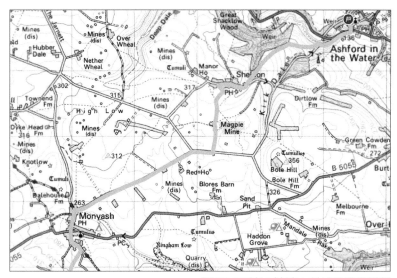

© Crown copyright and database rights 2021 OS 100065069

From the village green turn right into Chapel Street and then, at the next junction, turn right into Horse Lane signed Sheldon. At the end of the lane, turn right at the junction signed Ashford/Bakewell. After a short distance you will see the ruins of Magpie Mine on your left. Turn left along the track to the mine where you can explore the derelict buildings and read about the mine on the information boards. At the remains of the *Magpie Mine* you will find a cluster of buildings and mining relics. The lead mine has an interesting history, which is documented by the Peak District Mines Historical Society. The earliest record of the mine was in 1740. It closed and re-opened several times until its final closure in 1954. One of the fascinating facts concerns the rivalry with miners from other mines, which was often aggressive, leading to the "Magpie Murders". In 1833, miners from Magpie Mine lit fires underground to smoke out the rival miners which resulted in three of them being killed by suffocation. Although there was a subsequent murder trial of 24 miners, most were immediately freed and the remainder were not sentenced due to lack of intent and conflicting evidence. Allegedly, the widows of the 'murdered' miners put a curse on the mine and following this the mine never made a profit, and there were subsequent accidents and deaths.

The ruins of Magpie Mine

Cross the stile in the left-hand corner of the stone wall and cross the fields to reach several stone walls. Turn right here and follow the path through several wooden gates to Sheldon.

The mix of old houses and farms in the lovely village of **SHELDON** mainly originate from the 18th Century due to the success of the lead mining industry in the area. The exception, and perhaps surprisingly, is the Cock and Pullet pub which was built in 1995 and replaced the former Devonshire Arms next door which closed in 1971.

Turn right along the main road downhill out of the village and, just past the left-hand bend at Lower Farm, pass through the wooden gate. Walk straight across the field, maintaining height, to another gate in the middle of the field. The path from here contours round above the woods on your left and soon you will have a panoramic view with Ashford-in-the-Water down below. Cross the stile in the stone wall between the woods and the hedge and then continue downhill, bearing right away from the woods until you meet the river, then turn right and through a wooden gate. Turn left on the lane and then right along the main road until you reach the bridge across the river into Ashford-in-the-Water.

River Wye at Ashford-in-the-Water

River Wye

ASHFORD IN THE WATER
── TO ──
BUXTON

START	Ashford in the Water
FINISH	Buxton
DISTANCE	14.5 miles (23.3Km)
ASCENT	2,675 ft. (815m)
MAP	OS Explorer OL24
TERRAIN	Through woodland, dales, riverside paths, a former railway track and through fields
REFRESHMENTS	Refreshments and toilets at Miller's Dale

Ashford in the Water is a picturesque village, with many old cottages, which is situated on the River Wye, just two miles from Bakewell. The medieval bridge, the Sheep Wash Bridge, straddles the river and there is a good chance that you will see large trout swimming here. The packhorse bridge has its name because sheep used to be washed here before shearing.

Cross the bridge over the River Wye then cross the main A6 road and turn right. Walk up the lane towards Sheldon on the left. Where the lane bends to the left, by a small weir in the

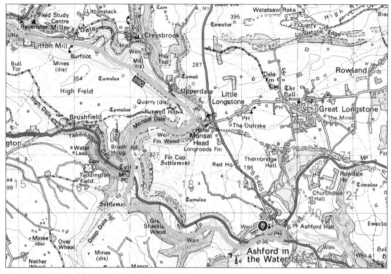

© Crown copyright and database rights 2021 OS 100065069

Ashford Bobbin Mill

river, take the footpath on the right through two gates and walk alongside the river. Pass through a wooden gate and walk straight on at a signpost, then cross a stile and walk straight on past an old water mill. Ashford Bobbin Mill was first a bone mill which produced fertiliser and later became a timber mill. You will also notice another building near the river which was a pumping house that used to supply water to the village of Sheldon which is around 500 feet above the river.

Monsal Dale

Bear left at the weir and immediately turn right on the footpath into Great Shacklow Wood. At the next signpost walk straight ahead to follow for White Lodge then pass through a wooden gate and turn right on the path downhill following for White Lodge/Deepdale. At the next signpost bear right downhill following the sign for White Lodge/Monsal Dale. Cross the stile in the stone wall and turn right on the path following the sign White Lodge/Monsal Dale, then pass through a gate in a stone wall and walk to the left-hand corner of White Lodge car park. Cross the A6 road and pass through a gap in the wall by a footpath sign and follow the path down to cross a small stream and a stile. Bear right following the sign for Monsal Head and follow the clear path ahead along Monsal Dale.

Walking through the lovely Monsal Dale you will reach the point where the stunning Monsal Head comes into view where the River Wye passes underneath the iconic Headstone viaduct. Just before you reach the viaduct, look for the path on the left and walk steeply uphill to join the Monsal Trail. Once on top of the viaduct, if you look to the right, you will see the entrance to the Headstone Tunnel through which steam trains once made the journey along this former railway line. Following its closure in 1968, it was transformed into the popular Monsal Trail for walkers, cyclists, horse riders and wheelchair users. The tunnel (at 533 yards long is the longest of a series of tunnels on this former railway line) remained closed for safety reasons but was eventually re-opened in 2011 following its conversion as a route for recreational purposes.

Cressbrook Tunnel

Our route is left along the Trail following the sign for Upperdale and Cressbrook. Continue along Monsal Trail to Millers Dale station, passing through the Cressbrook Tunnel and the Litton Tunnel. You will see Cressbrook and then Litton Mill on your right.

Just prior to reaching the former Millers Dale railway station you will walk across a viaduct which stands 80 feet above the River Wye, and is adjacent to a second viaduct which was opened in 1905 to provide additional capacity to serve the development of this once important railway junction.

MILLERS DALE railway station, built in 1863, was an important junction where passengers for Buxton joined or left the trains between London and Manchester and it was unusually large for a rural location, even having a post office on the platform. The station had an interesting history, because of its significance to Midland Railway and the passengers who used it, and it is fascinating to read about this. Redundant since the 1960s, the former station now serves as a car park, café and toilets for recreational users of the Monsal Trail.

From Miller's Dale the track passes a short stretch between rows of trees to shortly reach a bridge. Just before you reach the bridge, turn right on the path down steps signed Chee Dale then follow the path right alongside the river.

River Wye at Cheedale

Chee Dale is part of the River Wye Site of Special Scientific Interest and you may wish to slow your pace on this part of the walk to experience this unique environment. The deep sided limestone gorge is home to various species of trees, wild flowers and birds many of which you might see as you walk along the riverside path. In places the high cliffs hang over the path and you will need to cross the stepping stones beneath these.

Continue along the stony riverside path, cross the stepping stones and then cross the wooden footbridge. At the junction of paths, continue straight on by the riverside signed Blackwell Mill down stone steps and cross a wooden footbridge. Cross more stepping stones, pass under the railway bridge, cross a stile and continue on the riverside path.

Stepping stones at Cheedale

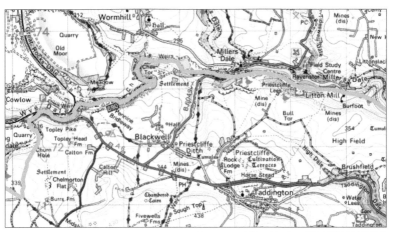

© Crown copyright and database rights 2021 OS 100065069

Pass under another railway bridge and, when you reach a row of cottages, turn left over the footbridge and then turn right and walk along the riverside track signed Wye Vale until you reach the car park by the A6 road. Cross the main road and walk up the path alongside the quarry access road.

Stepping stones at Cheedale

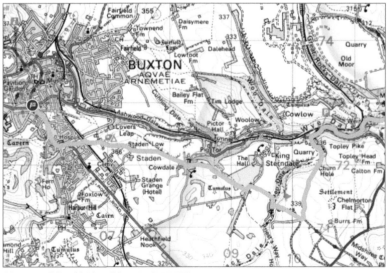

© Crown copyright and database rights 2021 OS 100065069

Once past the quarry look carefully for a wooden gate on your right and pass through it, then follow the path uphill signed Deepdale Alternative Route (the path to Deepdale is closed for restoration). At the top, cross a stile and follow the path bearing right across a field to reach a grass track. Walk along this to where it becomes a stone track and turn right at the junction, then shortly cross a stile on the right to pass through several fields descending into the steep-sided Deepdale. Follow the path steeply on the other side of the dale and walk through the fields to emerge on the road at King Sterndale. Turn left and then almost immediately right through fields signed Midshires Way until, just past the farm you will meet the road in the hamlet of Cowdale. Turn right and then almost immediately left through a gap in the stone wall, over a stile and through a gate. Walk through fields to the small hamlet of Staden. Bear right at the junction and follow the path through fields, pass the caravan and camping site and pass under the viaduct to reach the road. Turn left along the road to shortly meet the main road which will take you to the centre of Buxton.

Deepdale

Fernilee Reservoir

BUXTON
TO
WHALEY BRIDGE

START	Buxton
FINISH	Whaley Bridge
DISTANCE	8.6 miles (13.9Km)
ASCENT	1,227 ft. (374m)
MAP	OS Explorer OL24
TERRAIN	Initially on roads followed by moorland, and finally alongside reservoirs and the River Goyt.
REFRESHMENTS	Food and drink are available in Buxton where there are cafes, pubs and restaurants and shops selling food and drink. No refreshments then until arrival at Whaley Bridge.

Buxton is a thermal spa town (famous for its spring water) which is a popular tourist destination. It has stunning Georgian and Victorian buildings, including the Georgian Crescent and Buxton Opera House, and the beautiful unique Pavilion Gardens which date back to 1871.

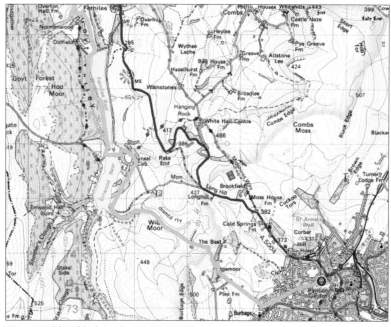

© Crown copyright and database rights 2021 OS 100065069

Wild Moor near Buxton

Starting in the centre of Buxton, walk along St. John's Road passing Buxton Pavilion and after walking for just over a half mile, where the road bends to the left, turn right into Bishops Lane and continue, passing Plex Lodge. Just past Yew Tree Cottage, the road rises steeply passing Top Lodge. Just past here, look carefully for the gap in the stone wall on the left and pass through, walking up the steep path, initially through trees and then bearing right towards the top corner of the wood. Pass through the wooden gate in the stone wall and follow the path bearing right onto moorland, and then shortly bearing left over a small patch of marshland. On reaching a small cairn, the views over Wild Moor are spectacular and a great contrast to the suburbs of Buxton. At this point the path bears right downhill and alongside a broken stone wall. On reaching a junction of paths you will see the old railway tunnel to your left, whilst and the former railway track contours round to the right.

A tunnel formerly used by Cromford & High Peak Railway

The track approaching Fernilee Reservoir

The Cromford & High Peak Railway track over Wildmoorstone Brook valley was completed in 1831 and was used to transport minerals and other goods through this bleak environment. The 33-mile railway connected the Cromford Canal with the Peak Forest Canal in Whaley Bridge.

Our route is almost straight ahead down the valley signed Wildmoorstone Brook. The path continues down the valley crossing several wooden footbridges. At the bottom you will reach a junction of paths where you turn right along the track signed Errwood Bunsal. Further down, cross a track coming from your right and continue straight across, maintaining this height above the reservoir. Follow the track through gaps in the trees and onto the road at the end. Turn left downhill and follow the road over the dam.

ERRWOOD RESERVOIR was the second of two reservoirs built in the Goyt Valley (the other one being Fernilee Reservoir) which was constructed by the Stockport Water Corporation and opened in 1968. It provides drinking water for Stockport and its surrounding areas, and it holds 4,215 million litres of water. The building of Errwood Reservoir resulted in the demise of the picturesque hamlet of Goyt's Bridge and the demolition of about twenty farms and cottages.

FERNILEE RESERVOIR, its slightly larger neighbour, was completed in 1937, taking five years to build. As with the construction of many reservoirs, a thriving community was lost. Many farms, a paint works, a gunpowder factory, a railway, a Victorian mansion, coal mines, a quarry, and a school that once occupied this tranquil and picturesque valley became the victims of development. The largest employer, the Fernilee gunpowder mill, employed over 100 men and apparently accidental explosions were a hazard of the job, some of these resulting in fatalities.

Fernilee Reservoir

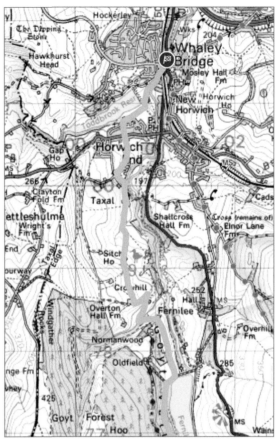

© Crown copyright and database rights 2021 OS 100065069

At the end of the dam leave the road and take the path by the large tree turning immediately right through the gate by the signpost for "Fernilee Reservoir", then shortly pass through another gate down to meet a track alongside the reservoir. After a while the path rises up steps away from the reservoir where you turn right on a broad track following the sign for "Fernilee" towards the dam. As you will see, the forest has been decimated due to essential felling, as a result of an outbreak of the tree disease Phytophthora Ramorum which has affected the Larch and Sweet Chestnut trees that stood here. It is a sad sight. Turn right onto a minor road and when you reach the corner of the dam, turn left along a stone track. Pass through a wooden gate by the house and continue straight ahead downhill through another gate and following the path right over the stream. Walk up the minor road on the left of Madscar Farm and continue on this road. At Overton Hall Farm turn right and follow the track straight ahead past the farm. Stay on the track until you reach the hamlet of Taxal and, immediately after passing the church, take the footpath on the right between trees to meet a minor road. Walk straight across onto the path and follow it across open ground towards houses and to a main road. Cross this into Reddish Lane and walk straight ahead at the end and follow it round to a footpath towards the corner of the dam. Walk to the left of the skateboard park and down the path passing the dam and the children's playground on your left. At the bottom turn left and walk over the bridge and follow the road into Whaley Bridge.

Taxal Church

Lyme Hall Estate

WHALEY BRIDGE
── TO ──
STOCKPORT

START	Whaley Bridge
FINISH	Stockport
DISTANCE	14 miles (22.6Km)
ASCENT	1,411 ft. (430m)
MAPS	OS Explorer OL1/O S Explorer 277
TERRAIN	The first mile is alongside a road followed by moorland and into Lyme Park. It then follows a canal towpath before crossing a golf course to reach the Middlewood Way then follows the River Goyt back to Stockport.
REFRESHMENTS	Food and drink are available in Whaley Bridge at shops, cafes and pubs and there is a refreshment kiosk and café in Lyme Park, then a refreshment kiosk at the Macclesfield Canal.

The town of **Whaley Bridge** on the River Goyt, situated 16 miles (26 km) southeast of Manchester, developed significantly during the Industrial Revolution when cotton mills became the main industry. Nowadays it is a tourist town with independent shops, pubs, restaurants and cafes. The Peak Forest Canal, which you walked along on the first day of the route, ends here in Whaley Bridge; it divides just outside the town turning east to Buxworth Basin and turning west to Marple. The canal formerly had great significance and the Transhipment Warehouse was once a key transfer station for limestone shipped across the UK. Whaley Bridge has been the victim of heavy rainfall. In 1872 it suffered a massive flood and more recently, in 2019, when flooding caused damage to the dam at **Toddbrook Reservoir**, and it was believed that there was a great chance of the dam collapsing and flooding Whaley Bridge and some surrounding areas. As a result, around 1,500 residents were evacuated and there was a multi-agency effort to pump water out of the reservoir to make it 'safe' before subsequent repair work could start.

Canal boats at Whaley Bridge

Subject to planning permission, the Canal & River Trust is hoping that the reservoir can be re-opened to the public in early 2024. The plan was for the Peak Way to use the footpaths alongside the reservoir, but in view of the potential closure of these paths and surrounding roads, the route has been changed. Although the first mile is uphill along a road, the effort is worthwhile for the views that you will enjoy from Whaley Moor.

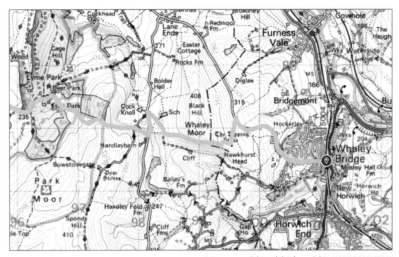

© Crown copyright and database rights 2021 OS 100065069

Leave the main road by the sign for the railway station into Reservoir Road under the railway bridge and immediately turn right on Whaley Lane. Follow the road uphill passing all the houses and the junction with Start Lane. When you have passed the last building on the left there are trees planted on the left-hand side and the road bends to the right. Just past the trees on the left-hand side, about 1 mile from the start, you will see a sign "Public footpath to Bowstonegate and Lyme Park" near a gate and stile. Cross the stile and follow the grassy path uphill in a southerly direction passing the marker post. The path ahead is clear across Whaley Moor and you will cross a stile, then a wooden footbridge, a stone wall stile, a stile by a metal gate, and then down to meet the track at the bottom where you turn right.

Walk ahead to meet the drive in the grounds of High Peak School (formerly a hotel) and walk down the drive to reach Mudhurst Road. Cross the road and follow the lane by the sign "Dissop Head Farm". Just after passing the farm on your left and Hill View House on your right, pass through a gate by a footpath sign on your right. Walk uphill and cross the next stile and then the stile on your left. Turn right and follow the path up to the top just left of the trees on the skyline. Cross the stile in the stone wall at the top and ignore the ladder stile on your right, continuing downhill with the wall on your right. You will now have extensive views of Manchester and the Cheshire plain. Further down, ignore the path veering left and continue by the wall to reach a ladder stile by a gate. Cross here and continue along the track to pass through a gate to meet the drive. Turn left in front of Lyme Hall and follow the path down to the car park.

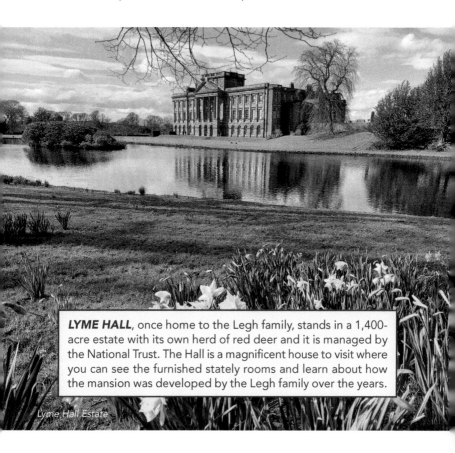

LYME HALL, once home to the Legh family, stands in a 1,400-acre estate with its own herd of red deer and it is managed by the National Trust. The Hall is a magnificent house to visit where you can see the furnished stately rooms and learn about how the mansion was developed by the Legh family over the years.

Lyme Hall Estate

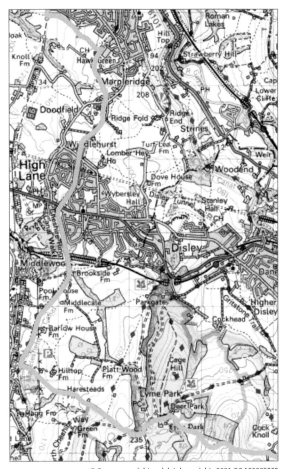

© Crown copyright and database rights 2021 OS 100065069

From the refreshment kiosk, follow the road alongside the car park and at the end follow the road to the right crossing the cattle grid. Walk uphill for a short distance until you reach a fork in the road and follow the right-hand track continuing right alongside the stone wall. You will see extensive views of Cheshire and Manchester. Continue downhill and pass through a wooden gate by a house. The track becomes rougher as you pass Haresteads Farm until you reach the bridge over the canal.

The **MACCLESFIELD CANAL** is over 27 miles long and runs from its junction with the Peak Forest Canal in Marple to its junction with the Trent & Mersey Canal at Kidsgrove. It opened in 1831 and was built to serve the mills, mines and quarries of the Marple, Poynton, Bollington, Macclesfield and Congleton areas as well as to provide a link from Manchester to the Potteries and Midlands.

Macclesfield Canal

Cross the bridge and turn immediately right on to the canal towpath passing the boatbuilders and the Trading Post refreshment kiosk. Continue along the towpath for almost 3 miles. Just before bridge no.4 (with the large mill building on the right) look carefully for the Marple Golf Club sign on the left and walk onto the course here. Follow the marker posts starting in a westerly direction and then north west towards trees. The path passes briefly between trees and then along the right-hand edge of the course, then back into a wood with houses across on the right side. It then emerges along the edge of the golf course again to meet a stile in the corner.

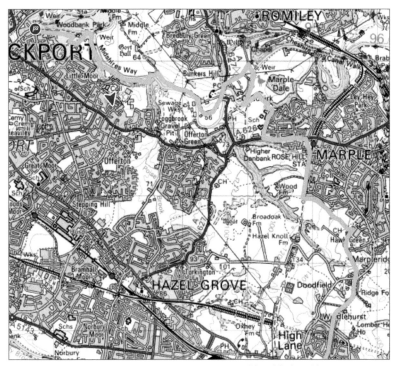

© Crown copyright and database rights 2021 OS 100065069

The **MIDDLEWOOD WAY** was a former railway line running 11 miles from Marple to Macclesfield between 1869 and 1970. Now it is a recreational facility for walkers, joggers, cyclists and horse riders.

Cross the stile and turn right onto the Middlewood Way then walk straight ahead for about a half mile to the end where you turn right on the road and walk up to the main road. Cross at the pedestrian crossing opposite the shop and turn left. Turn into the second road (Marple Hall Drive) and walk to the bottom of this road where it bends left. At this point walk straight on to the open land and follow the path round to the right as indicated by the sign for Stockport Centre. Pass the school sports fields

River Goyt near Chadkirk

River Goyt near Woodbank Park

on the left and at the junction of paths, follow the path down to the right to reach the river Goyt. Follow the riverside path then turn left over the bridge. At the junction of paths turn left to join the road a few yards ahead. You may recognise this road which you walked down on your first day. Walk to the end, turn left at the main road, cross at the pedestrian crossing then walk to the corner and turn right on the track towards Chadkirk Kennels. Follow the track until you reach signpost 517 indicating Midshires Way. You have the option to walk straight ahead here and retrace your steps from the first day if you wish, but the route turns left here down to the river and over the bridge. The path turns left uphill and then doubles round to the right. Look carefully for a white faintly painted arrow on a tree and follow the path in a westerly direction to reach Offerton Cricket Club pavilion. Follow the path to the right of the pavilion and through woodland above the river until you reach the path at the end. Turn left here and follow the path uphill to Woodbank Park where you started the walk.

CONGRATULATIONS

You have now completed the Peak Way long distance trail.

View of Edale Valley from the top of Jacob's Ladder

HAYFIELD
—— TO ——
EDALE

ALTERNATIVE ROUTE

START	Hayfield
FINISH	Edale
DISTANCE	6.5 miles (10.5Km)
ASCENT	1,618 ft. (493m)
MAP	OS Explorer OL1
TERRAIN	Part of the walk is on road followed by rough stone tracks for most of the walk. It then follows a path through fields from Upper Booth to Edale.
REFRESHMENTS	Food and drink are available in Hayfield but there are no refreshments then until you reach Edale.

This is an alternative route from Hayfield to Edale which avoids Kinder Scout in the event that the weather is extremely bad on the day that you plan to walk Kinder. Although it still reaches a height of over 1,600 feet, the route is easy to follow.

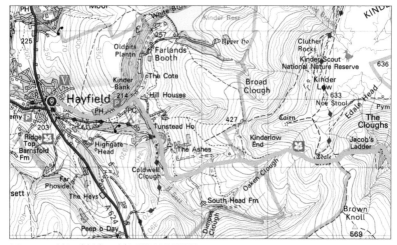

© Crown copyright and database rights 2021 OS 100065069

From the church in Hayfield look for the sign indicating 'one mile to the campsite' (Bank Street) and follow this to join Kinder Road. Look for the house on the left which has a blue plaque where actor, Arthur Lowe was born. Continue for almost one mile, passing the Sportsman Inn before arriving at Bowden Bridge car park where you can see another plaque, commemorating the endeavours and achievement by the mass trespass of 1932.

Plaque commemorating the Kinder Mass Trespass

Blue plaque at Arthur Lowe's former home

Cross the bridge opposite the car park and follow the road round to the left alongside the River Sett. When you reach the sign for Kinderstones/Tunstead House, bear right up the road. At the junction follow the track on the left over the cattle grid and on reaching a bend by the river walk straight ahead on the track in the field. You will shortly reach a gate where you pass over the stone stile alongside it, and follow the track uphill round to the left and past the farm house at Coldwell Clough. Then at the junction of tracks keep straight ahead uphill and pass through the wooden gate, continuing uphill on the stony track. You will see Mount Famine and South Head over on your right-hand side. Pass through a metal gate onto open moorland and continue along the track with the stone wall immediately on your left. Pass through another metal gate and follow the track round to the left.

Edale Cross

At approximately 3 miles from the start of the walk you will see Edale Cross (a medieval cross) on your left. From here the path continues downhill and then up to a junction of paths (signpost for Pennine Way going left). Pass through the wooden gate and walk downhill.

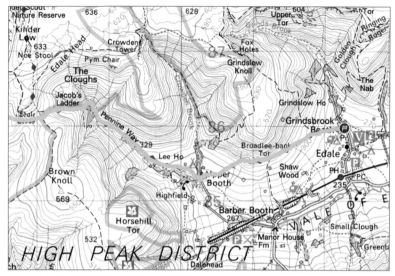

© Crown copyright and database rights 2021 OS 100065069

You will reach a sign "Public Footpath by Jacob's ladder" by a large stone cairn with a great view down the Edale Valley. At the bottom of Jacob's Ladder cross the stone bridge and pass through the wooden gate. The track ahead is obvious, passing several stiles and gates and through the farm to the end where you cross the stone bridge at Upper Booth. Turn left into the farmyard passing a wooden gate with a footpath sign and following the Pennine Way "Footpath to Edale" sign. Follow the track passing through several gates and stiles. Rushup Edge and the Great Ridge are on the opposite side of the Valley. The path eventually reaches a track with a signpost. Walk through the gate and turn right on the path and follow it alongside the stream to shortly reach Grindsbrook Booth (known as Edale).

Descent to Edale

The path towards Edale

PART

3

FACILITIES ALONG THE ROUTE

The table on pages 140 and 141 should help you in planning your walk each day. Many of the towns and villages have restaurants, cafes and pubs where you can get meals and drinks. However, it is important to note that, on some sections, you will need to stock up with refreshments that you will need along the way because there will be nothing available until you reach the destination.

Similarly, if you do need cash along the way you need to ensure that you have enough cash for your daily needs because of the irregular provision of banks and ATMs in rural areas, although Post Offices will facilitate cash withdrawals. Some Post Offices are located in other buildings such as the one at Bamford which is in the Anglers Rest pub, and some are only open on certain days each week; you can check the Post Office website (www.postoffice.co.uk/branch-finder). You will find though, that accommodation providers, restaurants, pubs and many cafes and shops accept debit/credit cards.

Mobile phone signals are inconsistent and you may find that you have a strong signal in some areas, but at times you will not have a network connection. Many of the public phone boxes that you see in rural areas have been converted into book swop and information facilities or defibrillator stations, but you will find public telephones in the main towns.

The table shows places that have dedicated toilet facilities but there are, of course, facilities in pubs, cafes etc. You can use most of the public toilets free of charge but very occasionally there is a minimum charge.

Section	Place	Meals	ATM	Post Office	Phone	Toilets	Food
1	Stockport	Y	Y	Y	Y	Y	Y
	Marple	Y	Y	Y	Y	Y	Y
	New Mills	Y	Y	Y	Y	Y	Y
2	Hayfield	Y	Y	Y		Y	Y
	Edale	Y		Y		Y	Y
3	Hope	Y	Y	Y	Y	Y	Y
4	Bamford	Y		Y		Y	Y
5	Grindleford	Y		Y			
6	Baslow	Y		Y		Y	Y
	Chatsworth	Y				Y	Y
	Edensor						Y
	Bakewell	Y	Y	Y	Y	Y	Y
7	Rowsley	Y		Y			Y
	Darley Bridge	Y					
	Matlock	Y	Y	Y	Y	Y	Y
8	Matlock Bath	Y		Y		Y	Y
	Cromford	Y		Y		Y	Y
	Middleton Top Visitor Centre					Y	Y
	Ashbourne	Y	Y	Y	Y	Y	Y
9	Ashbourne Cycle Hire					Y	Y
	Dovedale Car Park					Y	Y
	Milldale					Y	Y
	Hartington	Y		Y		Y	Y

Section	Place	Meals	ATM	Post Office	Phone	Toilets	Food
10	Hartington Signal Box					Y	Y
	Parsley Hay Cycle Hire					Y	Y
	Monyash	Y				Y	Y
	Sheldon	Y					
	Ashford-in-the-Water	Y		Y		Y	Y
11	Millers Dale					Y	Y
	Buxton	Y	Y	Y	Y	Y	Y
12	Whaley Bridge	Y	Y	Y	Y	Y	Y
13	Lyme Park					Y	Y
	Higher Poynton Marina						Y
	High Lane		Y	Y		Y	Y
	Stockport	Y	Y	Y	Y	Y	Y
14	Edale	Y			Y	Y	Y

KEY

MEALS: Pub/restaurant or café where you can get an evening meal

ATM: Automated Teller Machine where you can withdraw cash

Post Office offering cash withdrawal (some are in other buildings and some open part-time)

PHONE: Public payphone

TOILETS: Public Toilets

FOOD: Shop, kiosk or café where you can buy refreshments

Accommodation

Once you have decided how long you intend to take to walk the Peak Way (including any rest days and/or stops to visit tourist attractions) you will need to book your accommodation. The Peak District is very popular with tourists and so it advisable to book well in advance. Also, please be aware that not all providers take single-night stays and there is a minimum two or three nights stay at some accommodation. A list of accommodation providers will be available through the Peak Way website soon (www.peakwaywalk.com) which includes hotels, pubs, bed & breakfast/guesthouses, youth hostels and campsites. You can either contact accommodation providers directly to make your bookings and discuss your requirements, or you can use online booking services such as that provided by Marketing Peak District and Derbyshire (www.visitpeakdistrict.com).

Where providers do not take single night bookings, it may be feasible to stay for two or three nights and use transport to return to your accommodation and to get to your next start point on the following day(s). Some accommodation providers are "hiker friendly" and may offer to collect you at the end of your day's walk, or take you to your start point the next day, but you should check this, if necessary, when you book accommodation. Some may even take your luggage to the next accommodation that you have booked. There is usually, although not always, an extra charge for this service, but it may be well worth paying for. Some providers also provide facilities such as drying rooms for wet boots and clothing and some will provide packed lunches whilst others will not.

Baggage Transfer

Brigantes Walking Holidays can provide a baggage transfer service for the Peak Way, so if you just want to carry your rucksack and walking gear each day (which is a good idea on a long-distance walk), Brigantes can transport your other baggage to your accommodation so that it will be there when you arrive after your walk each day. You can contact Brigantes by phone 01756 770402 or visit their website www.brigantesenglishwalks.com.

Tourist Attractions and Events

The Peak District offers a great variety of tourist attractions from caves and historical houses to breweries and museums. There are also many fabulous events throughout the year. So, if you have time to plan a few extra days, you can find out about the full range by visiting the tourism website www.visitpeakdistrict.com or by contacting any of the Tourist Information Centres.

The Peak Way passes through the grounds of two major tourist attractions, Chatsworth House and Estate and Lyme Hall & Park. These two magnificent historic houses, and their gardens and grounds are well worth visiting and, if you have time, and I highly recommend that you build in time to visit them.

Useful Addresses & Web Sites
Tourist Information Centres (near the route)

There are 10 Tourist Information Centres either on the Peak Way or very near to the route and these are listed below. They offer a significant amount of local information and the staff are very knowledgeable and helpful. They can provide information and advice on accommodation, ticket sales, transport, attractions and events.

HIGH PEAK JUNCTION VISITOR CENTRE
off Lea Road, Cromford, Matlock DE4 5HN
Tel. 01629 533298

MATLOCK BATH INFORMATION POINT
Peak District Mining Museum, The Pavilion, Matlock Bath, Matlock DE4 3NR
Tel. 01629 583834

CASTLETON VISITOR CENTRE
Buxton Road, Castleton, Hope Valley S33 8WN
Tel. **01629 816572**

UPPER DERWENT VISITOR CENTRE
Fairholmes, Bamford, Hope Valley S33 0AQ
Tel. **01433 650953**

MOORLAND VISITOR CENTRE
Fieldhead, Edale, Hope Valley S33 7ZA
Tel. **01433 670207**

BUXTON VISITOR CENTRE
The Pump Room, The Crescent, Buxton SK17 6BH
Tel. **01298 214577**

ASHBOURNE VISITOR INFORMATION CENTRE
Town Hall Yard, Ashbourne DE6 1ES
Tel. **01335 343666**

MANIFOLD VALLEY INFORMATION POINT
Hulme End, Hartington, SK17 0EZ
Tel. **01538 483741**

BAKEWELL VISITOR CENTRE
Old Market Hall, Bridge Street, Bakewell DE45 1DS
Tel. **01629 816558**

MATLOCK VISITOR INFORMATION POINT
Peak Rail Shop, Matlock Railway Station, Matlock DE4 3NA
Tel. **01629 761103**

Other

YOUTH HOSTEL ASSOCIATION
Trevelyan House, Dimple Road, Matlock DE4 3YH
www.yha.co.uk

PEAK DISTRICT TOURISM
www.vistpeakdistrict.com